45 Fine & Fanciful Hats to Knit

Anna Zilboorg

Berets ◇ Toques ◇ Cones
Stars ◇ Pentagons ◇ and More

Lark Books

Editor: Dawn Cusick
Art/Production: Elaine Thompson
Photographer: Evan Bracken
Illustrators: Bobby Gold, Eric Stevens
Proofreader: Julia Brown

Library of Congress Cataloging-in-Publication Data
Zilboorg, Anna, 1933-
     45 fine & fanciful hats to knit : berets, toques, cones, stars,
pentagons, and more / Anna Zilboorg.
       p. cm.
    Includes index.
    ISBN 1-57990-000-3
    1. Knitting--Paterns. 2. Hats. I. Title.
TT825.Z55   1997
746.43'20432--dc21   97-13130
                           CIP

10 9 8 7 6 5 4 3 2 1

First Edition

Published by Lark Books
50 College St.
Asheville, NC 28801, USA

Copyright ©1997 Anna Zilboorg

Distributed by Random House, Inc., in the United States,
   Canada, the United Kingdom, Europe, and Asia

Distributed in Australia by Capricorn Link (Australia) Pty Ltd.,
   P.O. Box 6651, Baulkham Hills Business Centre, NSW 2153,
   Australia

Distributed in New Zealand by Tandem Press Ltd.,
   2 Rugby Rd., Birkenhead, Auckland, New Zealand

Printed in Hong Kong by Oceanic Graphic Printing Productions Ltd.

All rights reserved.

ISBN 1-57990-000-3

Dedication

For David, who wears these hats with panache.

Acknowledgements

My thanks first of all to Gina Halpern, painter and sculptor, who does not disdain the humble hat. She has inspired me by example and by her insistence that I needed **all** the colors. Next, I'm grateful to Elizabeth Zimmerman, from whom I learned to make berets, then other shapes. Her encouragement to experiment has been crucial for me as for so many once timid knitters. For the making of this book, I give thanks for my editor, Dawn Cusick, especially for her good cheer in dismal times. And I thank my friends who have urged me on, especially Mary Dashiell and Mary K. Wakeman. A special word of thanks to XRX, who through *Stitches* gave me a forum to try out these designs and directions, and through *Knitters Magazine* have aided, abetted, and encouraged me.

Sincere thanks are also extended to the following hat models: Mary Bracken, Leslie Lehner, Holly Lanning, Samantha Vandermeade, Gabrielle Vandermeade, Sara Chadwick, Wanda Dente, Shandy Haney, Patrick Doran, Laura Dover Doran, Will Albrecht, and Wesley Albrecht.

Contents

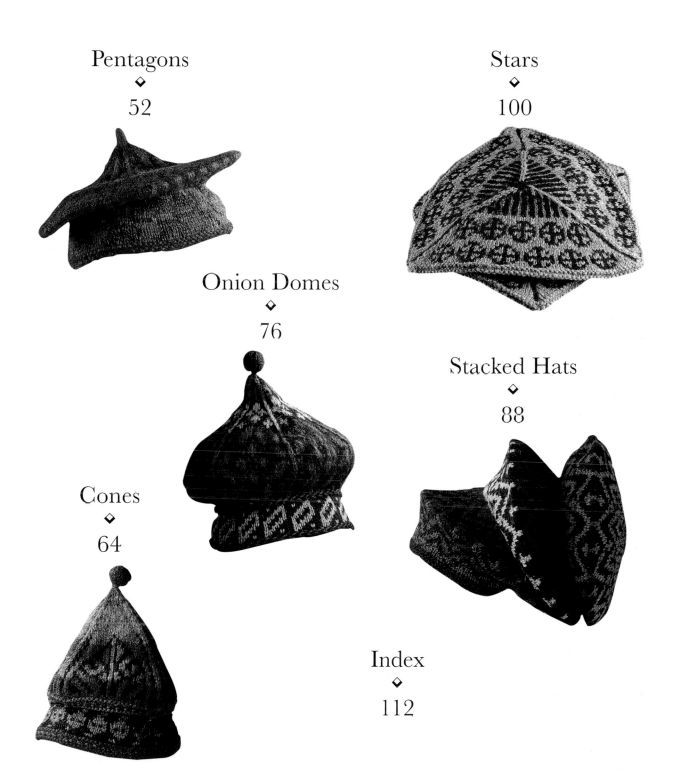

Introduction

Knitted wool hats are wonderful for many reasons. Everyone (at least everyone who lives in a temperate climate) should have at least one. They are warm and comfortable in the most miserable weather. When it's cold and rainy, they are positively comforting. And they can be squashed in a pocket without possibility of harm.

The one drawback to knitted wool hats seems to be that many people feel they do not look well in them, and when we don't look well, we don't feel well. I hope the hats in this book will solve this problem. In my years of doing craft shows, I have yet to see anyone who did not look well in one hat or another.

Choosing a hat is largely a matter of preference. Over and over again I have seen people drawn to just the hats that will look best on them, whether one would have predicted it or not. There are, however, several exceptions. People with small heads often feel they have to wear small hats, so they put on a toque or a cone and say, "See, I look awful in hats." Yet they look wonderful in a beret or a pentagon -- something that gives a frame to the face and thus enlarges the head.

Large heads often look well in middle-sized hats, not too tight and not too big and floppy. They tend to look especially nice in the Egyptian hat. Square faces look well in cones worn pointed up on top of the head. Long faces can happily wear stacked hats, bonnet-style. But in truth there are no rules. If you make what most appeals to you, the chances are it will look wonderful. And there are so many ways to wear each of these hats, you will surely find a way to style it that suits your spirit.

There is yet another reason for these hats. They are a happy sight for others to see when the sky is gray and the temperature frigid. Wearing cheerful, multicolored hats is a public service, easy to perform, and of incalculable value. I first realized this on a trip to the New England Aquarium in Boston with my son and his family. We were an ordinary family group, but strangers were smiling at us and nodding. People don't do this in Boston. On the subway trip home, all was explained when a woman asked if I had knit them. It was the hats that were making usually grim faces smile.

These hats have come to me over time from various sources and inspirations. I think of them as traveling hats. When I first started making berets, I carried them with me in a basket as I travelled. I sold them as I went, even as they came off the needles, in airports, on trains, even in a hotel lobby. They have also gone great distances: up a mountain in Nepal, to a fjord in Iceland, and down the London tube. One was even complimented in the Louvre. They have been a great gift to me in my own travel through life, so it is right for me to pass them on. Wooly hats are small things, but cheerful ones. I hope they will bring warmth and pleasure to those who knit them, those who wear them, and those who see them.

General Information, Instructions, and Techniques

The specific directions for each style of hat appear at the beginning of each chapter. Each hat is then shown in full color and illustrated with appropriate pattern charts. This general section contains instructions and descriptions that apply one way or another to all of the hats or to various ones in different sections. A quick review of these instructions before you begin working on a specific hat may prove helpful.

Materials
◆

About 4 ounces (112 g) various worsted weight yarns will make most of the hats in this book. The Angela hats will need about 5 ounces (140 g); the domes, stacks, and stars, about 6 ounces (168 g) each. To estimate how much of each color is necessary, count on 2 yards (1.8 m) of each color for each stranded round or 4 yards (3.6 m) for a single color round.

You will need a 16-inch (41 cm) circular needle and a set of double-pointed needles in a size that gives 5 stitches per inch (2.5 cm) in pattern. (For most knitters, stranded knitting is about a half stitch per inch tighter than single color stockinette stitch.) It is a good idea, though not absolutely necessary, to start the hat on a needle two or three sizes smaller than the one you use for the main knitting. You need the double-pointed needles for the top of the hats when you have decreased to where there are too few stitches to reach around 16 inches. Since you will be decreasing down to very few stitches, it is easier to use short needles; about 4 or 5 inches (10–13 cm) is ideal.

Sizes
◆

One hat will fit many different heads. Nevertheless, it will not fit all heads. These hats are sized for medium-headed adult women. For a particularly large head, they can be made of heavier yarn (worsted weight, as opposed to Dk) at 4.5 stitches per inch. For a child, 5.5 stitches per inch should work in most cases. For a really little one, use sport yarn. If you are making a hat for a very large man, you may want to add a whole section to the pattern. Instead of repeating a segment eight times, for instance, you would add sufficiently more stitches and repeat it nine times.

The Angela hat has directions for three different sizes. The others are not so easy to alter by a few stitches, since the patterns were drawn to fit into particular shapes. Fortunately, exact fit is not necessary in a knitted hat.

Charts
◆

The charts show the pattern to be worked and the shaping of each segment. Each square of the chart denotes one stitch. The background color is left blank and the contrasting color is indicated by a symbol. All charts are worked from the bottom (the first round) to the top (the last round). All charts are worked from right to left, the direction you are knitting. One segment of pattern is shown in each chart and is to be repeated around the hat. The number of repeats is indicated on the right-hand side of the chart by a number followed by an X. Thus, 6X means you repeat one row of the chart six times before moving up to the next row. Then you repeat that row six times before moving up to the next, and so on until the chart is completed.

When the next row of your chart has fewer stitches in it than the previous row, you must decrease where the chart decreases: on the right side, on the left side or, most frequently, on both sides. When the chart has more stitches, you must increase.

You will notice that in most charts there is a single stitch on the left side that rises straight up, independent of whether the rest of the chart is increasing or decreasing. This is the final stitch of each segment of pattern. It is neither increased nor decreased itself: the increases and decreases take place on either side of it, or, most frequently, on both sides of it. In the case of the double decrease (see below), this stitch is involved in the decrease, but it remains headed straight up because the stitches on both sides disappear behind it.

There are two charts given for each hat. One is the bottom, where the hat is started. The other shows the shaping of the top of the hat with the stitches decreasing, finally, to just one, two, or three in each segment.

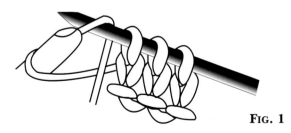

FIG. 1

Colors

◆

Many of these hats use quite a few colors, though for the most part there are only two colors in a round. (There are a few exceptions where there are three colors in a round, but it's just for one round.) The hats can be made with as few as two colors if you like, but they cannot be made with one color because there are more rows to an inch in single color knitting than there are in stranded knitting. If you want to make a solid-colored hat, you'll have to increase the number of rounds you knit. I've used lots of colors both for fun and to suggest that many leftover bits of yarn can go into making a splendid hat. I've changed the symbol on the charts for the pattern color whenever I've changed colors. When the background color changes, it's indicated by a bold line across the chart.

Technique

◆

Two kinds of increases are used: M1 and the lifted increase. The M1 is made by placing a halfhitch on the right-hand needle. That is, you pick up the yarn over your left index finger from back to front. Bring the right needle forward and use it to take the loop off the left index finger. This is a lot easier to do than say. (See Figure 1.)

The lifted increase is also harder to explain than do. Here you want to knit into the top of the next stitch on the preceding row. Look over your needles to the wrong side of the knitting. The top of the stitch of the preceding row forms a bump around the stitch on the needle. Insert the point of your right hand needle under this bump and knit a stitch. (See Figure 2A.) Then knit the stitch on the needle. (See Figure 2B.) One stitch has been almost invisibly increased.

You can increase in one color and knit the stitch in another, if that's what the chart indicates.

For decreasing you will have to know how to do a decrease that slants to the right, one that slants to the left, and one that decreases two stitches at a time with a third stitch between them remaining vertical. Most knitters are familiar with the right-slanting decrease: K2 together through the front of the sts. (See Figure 3.) The left-slanting decrease can be made by K2 tog through the back of the sts. This will twist the sts, however. To prevent twisting the sts, slip two, one at a time from the left-hand needle to the right. Then insert the left needle into the front of both sts and knit them together. (See Figure 4.) This is known as SSK in most directions.

Make the double decrease as follows: Slip 2 sts together from left needle as though you were going to decrease them. In other words, do not slip them one at a time. (See Figure 5A.) Knit the next st. Now slip the two sts slipped tog over the just-knit st.

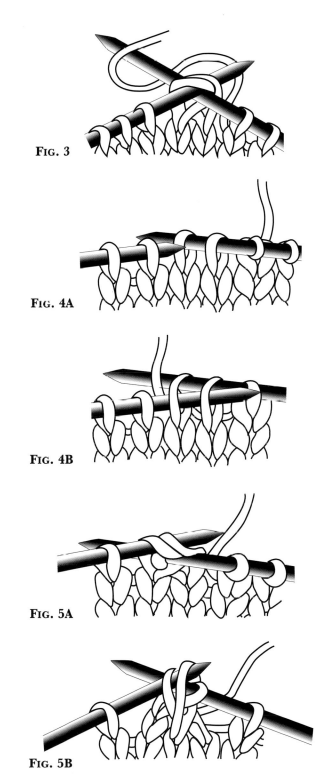

FIG. 3

FIG. 4A

FIG. 4B

FIG. 5A

FIG. 5B

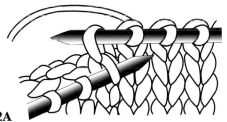

FIG. 2A

FIG. 2B

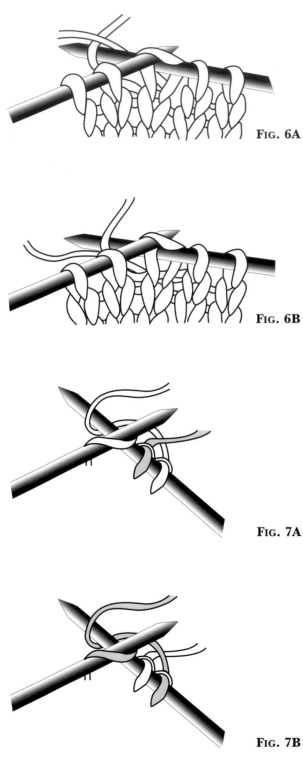

FIG. 6A

FIG. 6B

FIG. 7A

FIG. 7B

(See Fig. 5B.) The middle st stands in front, while the right and left sts are tucked in behind them.

You also need to know how to carry a pattern color over more than 5 or 6 sts and how to weave it in. Hold the yarn to be carried in your left hand, over your index finger. (This is presumably where you have it if you are knitting two-handed.) As you throw the yarn with your right hand, place the right hand needle under the left yarn for a few sts, then over it for the next few sts. (See Figure 6.) This is much simpler than twisting the yarns and less visible on the right side.

One other technique used in some of the hats is the bobble. There are many ways of making bobbles and any method will do. My favorite is K1, yo, K1, yo, K1 in one stitch. Turn and K back over these 5 sts. Turn and P back. Turn and K back. The bobble sts are on the L needle. With the R needle, pass the 2nd, 3rd, and 4th sts over the first st one by one. Knit the single st to complete the bobble.

Bands

◆

Some of the hat styles begin with 5 ridges of garter st. Most begin with a narrow band that is repeated before the top shaping. The three methods of making the narrow bands are interchangeable. Which you choose depends on which you like the look of at the moment or which technique you feel like doing. The techniques follow.

Band A

Work 1 ridge garter st (K1 rnd, P1 rnd). With CC, work 1 rnd, K1, sl1 (with yarn in back) and 1 rnd P1, sl1 (yarn in back). With MC, work 1 ridge garter st. This is the band I use most frequently.

Band B

The braided band is a bit more complicated. Rnd 1: K1A, K1B around. Now turn the work so that the wrong side (the purl side) is facing you. Bring the yarns to the back, pull out 2 or 3 yards (1.8 or 2.7 m) of each yarn from the balls, and prepare to work in the other direction. Rnd 2: K1B (the same color as on the previous rnd). Drop B. Bring A under B and K1A. DropA. Bring B under A and K1B. (See Figure 7A.) Continue in this way all around. The yarns will be twisting with each stitch you take — that's why you pulled out extra before you began. When you return to the beginning, begin taking the working yarn over the yarn of the last stitch instead of under. (See Figure 7B.) Continue around in this manner, untwisting the yarns as you go. When you get back to the beginning again, turn your work to the right side and there will be your braid. This band is a bit of a bother to do, but it's only two rnds of bother and it does look elegant.

Band C

This band is the easiest of all. It consists of three rnds of reverse stockinette st. That is, you can purl 3 rnds or you can turn your work and knit 3 rnds and then turn your work back again. I don't use it often, but sometimes I want a solid color on the bands, and sometimes I just feel lazy.

The Ball on Top of the Hat

◆

Many of the hats in this book are finished with a knitted ball on top. I prefer balls to any sort of pom-pom because they are neater and hold up better. (I also find them more pleasant to make.)

Elizabeth Zimmerman, mother of modern knitting, says the way to make a ball is to knit a tube on a few sts (in this case about 10). Roll up a tight little ball of yarn. Push it into the tube. Finish off the tube by running the end of yarn through the sts and pulling them tight. Then wrap the yarn several times around the base of the tube under the ball. This method works very well and anyone should feel free to use it.

I, on the other hand, like to shape my balls. I start with 8 sts. K one rnd on these 8 sts. Rnd 2: M1, K2 around (12sts). Rnd 3: K. Rnd 4. M1, K1 around (24 sts). Rnds 5 & 6: K. Rnd 7: K2 tog around (12sts). Rnd 8: K. Stop here and wind up a tight little ball of yarn. Push it into the sack you've been knitting. Rnd 9: K2 tog around (6 sts). Cut the yarn, leaving an 8-inch (20 cm) tail. Run this tail through the remaining sts and pull tight. Thread the tail onto a sharp needle and run it through the ball and out at its base, then wrap it several times around the base of the ball. Run the yarn back up through the ball and out. Cut the yarn off close to the ball.

These are called Angela hats after a friend who made one from polar fleece for my daughter. It looks quite different in knitting but it is still a wonderful hat. The Angela hat style is the only one in this collection made of straight pieces, so it's easily done by machine as well as by hand. Because of its simplicity, the size is easy to change. Toddler, child, and adult sizes are included. The strips and the hat bodies are all interchangeable on these hats.

Directions

On short, double-pointed needles, cast on 24 (28, 32) sts. Leave a tail long enough to sew the end of tube together. P1 rnd in background color. Work around in strip pattern for 16 (17, 18) inches (or as long as desired). Now, maintaining the pattern, work back and forth for 42 (48, 54) rows. (You will have to keep the sts on two or three needles for the first inch or so.) Then begin working around again and continue for the same length as the other side. P1 rnd in background color. Cast off, leaving an end long enough to sew the tube closed.

    With ground color and 16-inch (41 cm) circular needle, pick up 1 st every row on the side of the strip worked flat. When you finish picking up one side, continue picking up the other side. This should give you 84 (96, 108) sts on the needle. Follow the hat chart until it is completed. With the ground color, K17 (19, 21) rnds plain.

    Cast off. Roll the bottom of the hat so the purl side shows. (It will roll this way naturally.)

Blocking
No difficulty with this one. Steam the hat flat and roll up the bottom while it's still warm.

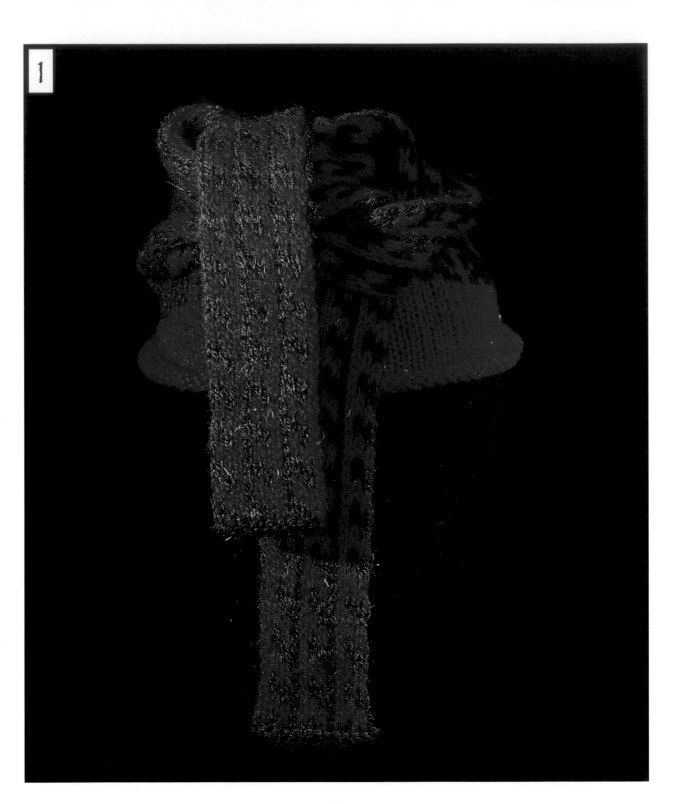

6(7,8)x

strip

7(8,9)x

hat

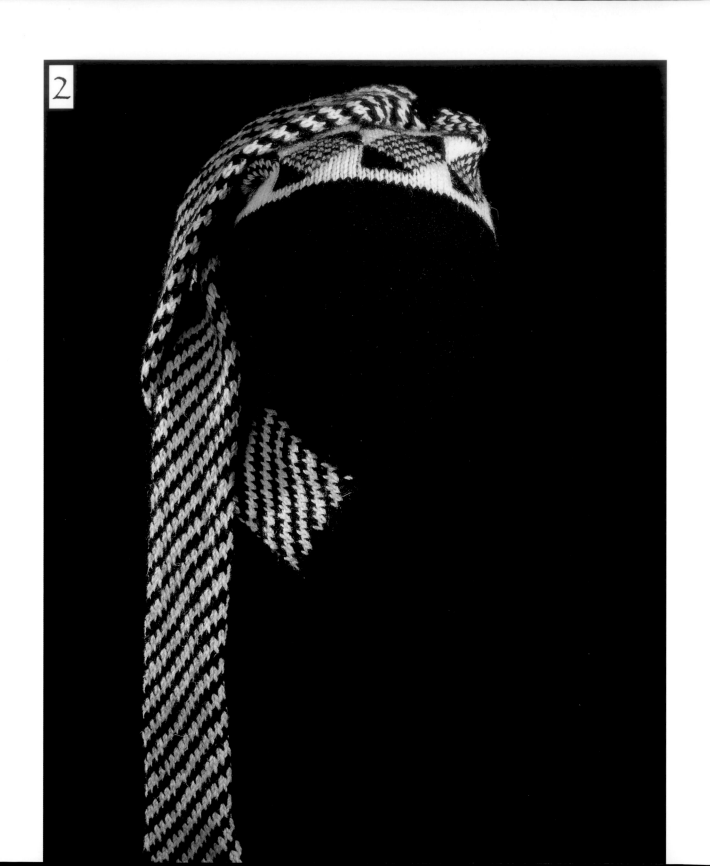

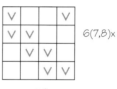

strip

6(7,8)x

7(8,9)x

hat

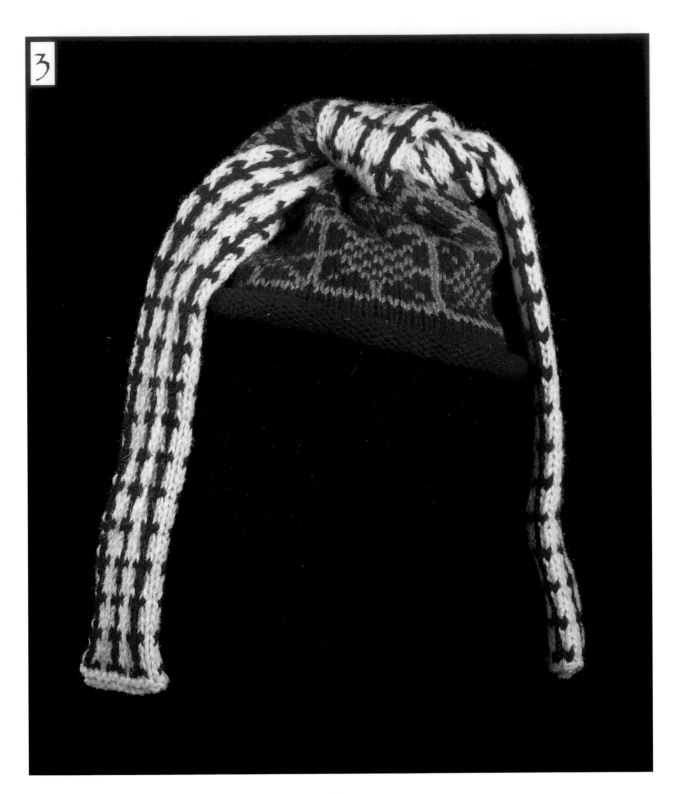

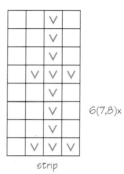

6(7,8)x

strip

7(8,9)x

hat

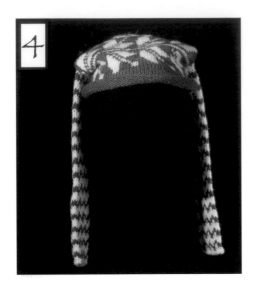

(See photo on page 12.)

hat 7(8,9)

7(8,9)x

strip

6(7,8)x

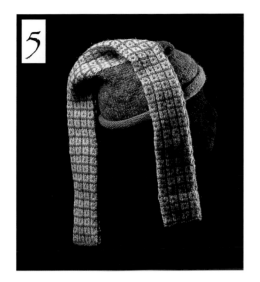

(See photo on page 12.)

6(7,8)x

strip

7(8,9)x

hat

erets are some of the most familiar knitted hats. They are quite
simple to make, look well on
almost everyone, and are eminently practical.
They easily fit in a raincoat pocket, providing
warmth and comfort in occasional showers,
and they look cheery on dreary days. Berets
certainly do not need to be worn on an angle
in the French manner; straight back and cov-
ering the ears is my personal preference.

The only difficulty with knitted berets is
that, traditionally, they are knit at a very fine
gauge, necessitating a prodigious number of
stitches. So here are a few berets knit with
worsted-weight yarn in a variety of patterns.

Directions

For the bottom band, cast on 84 sts on smaller
16-inch (41 cm) circular needle. Work 5 ridges
garter st. Count the cast on as the first row. You
can either knit back and forth and sew the band
together when done, or you can work it circularly,
purling every other round. When there are 5
ridges on the right side, increase to 144 sts.
{* (K1. M1) 3X, K1. Repeat from * to the
last 5 sts. K the last 5 sts.}

Change to larger needle. Follow the charts
for the beret of choice, beginning at the bottom
of the straight chart and repeating around the
hat. The number of times the pattern must be
repeated is indicated beside the chart. When the
straight chart is finished, move to the shaped one.

All of these berets use the double decrease.
When the charts are finished, run the end of the
yarn through the remaining sts and pull tight.
Finish the ends inside and sew up band.

Blocking

To block the hat, you will need a circular plate about
11 inches (28 cm) in diameter or something similar.
Pull the hat over the circle and steam it, starting at
the top and working from the center out. Turn the
hat over and steam the bottom, pulling it in.

Note: If you cannot find anything circular of
suitable size, wet down the hat and roll it in a
towel to remove excess water. Lay the hat flat in a
circle, pinning down the turned edge as often as
possible. (Knitted hats really don't want to stretch
when they're dry, so be sure to wet the hat before
pinning and steaming.)

6x

8x

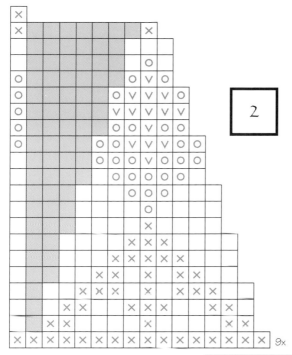

2

9x

12x

3

12x

* dec. 1st on this rnd (143 sts remain)

13x

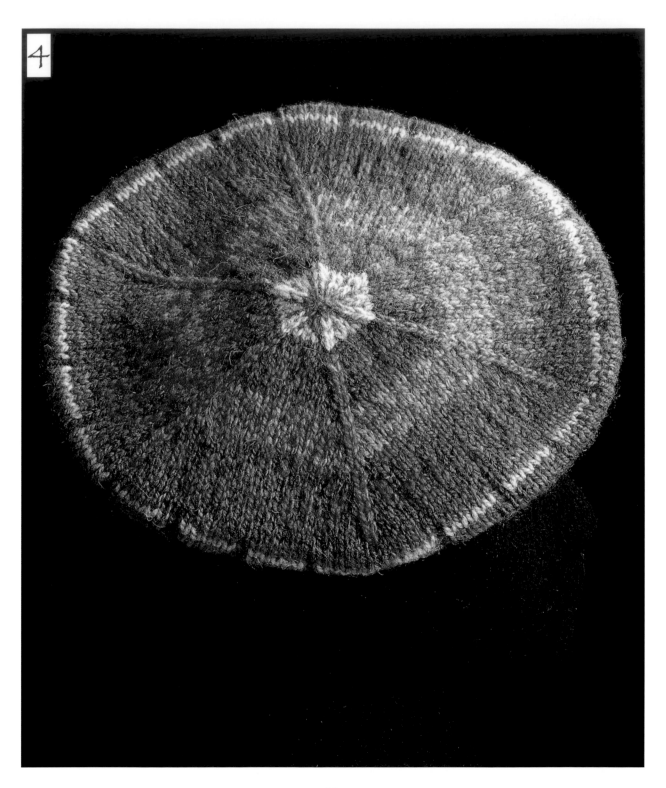

6x

12x

12x

12x

Toques

y dictionary *(The American Heritage Dictionary of the English Language)* defines a toque as a small, brimless, close-fitting woman's hat. The hats I've given here differ from most close-fitting, contemporary hats in two ways. First, the top is separated from the bottom by a band that causes the top to lie flat. Second, the bottom is slightly tapered. Tapering the bottom limits the patterns that can be used but makes for a more graceful, comfortable fit.

Directions

On smaller, 16-inch (41 cm) circular needle, cast on 96 sts. Work desired band. (Band A is shown on hat #1; band B on hat #s 2, 3, and 4; and band C on hat #5).

Follow the bottom chart, using a lifted increase where increases are shown.

When you have completed the chart, work the band again (now on 120 sts).

Work the top chart. Use the double decrease on hat #s 1, 2, and 4. Use R- slanting dec at beginning and L-slanting dec at ending of chart segments on hat #4. Use R-slanting dec at end of chart segment on hat #5.

When the chart is finished, run end of yarn through remaining sts and pull tight.

Blocking

The bottom of this hat can be steamed over the tip of an ironing board or sleeve board. The top can be steamed over a 9-inch (23 cm) plate or a 9-inch circle of Masonite or cardboard.

6x

Top

6x

Bottom

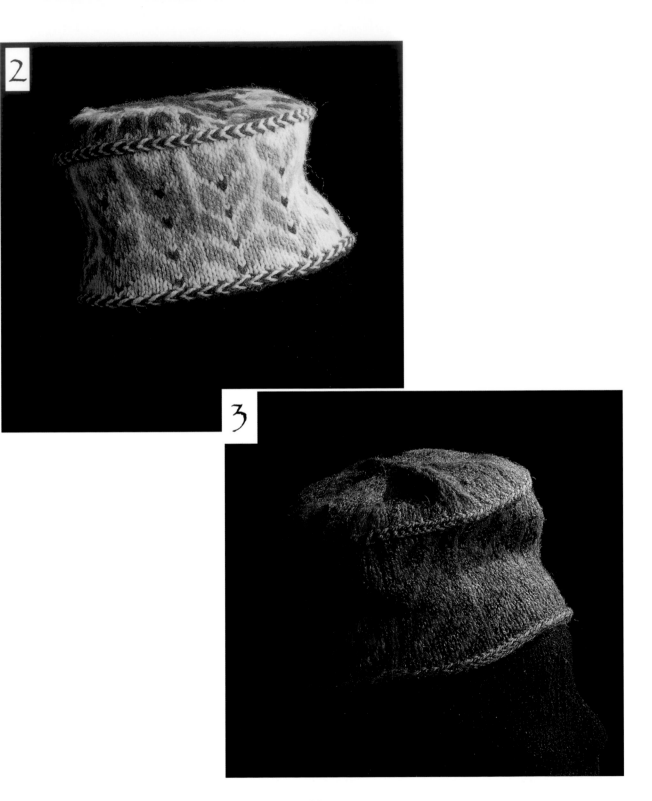

2

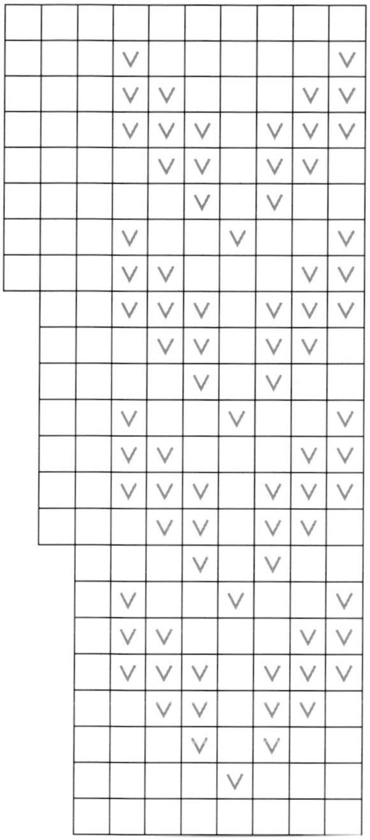

Bottom

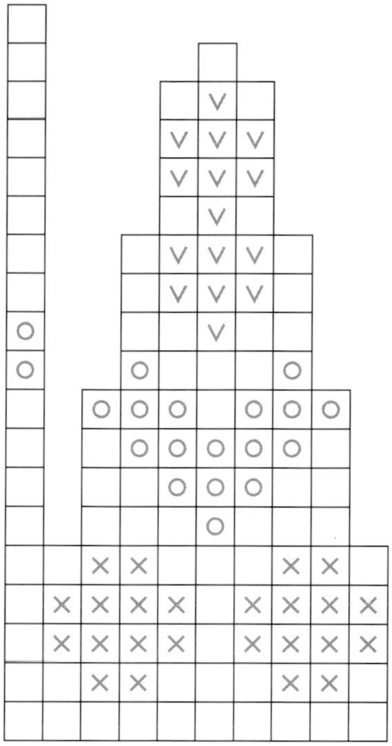

12

Top

12x

3

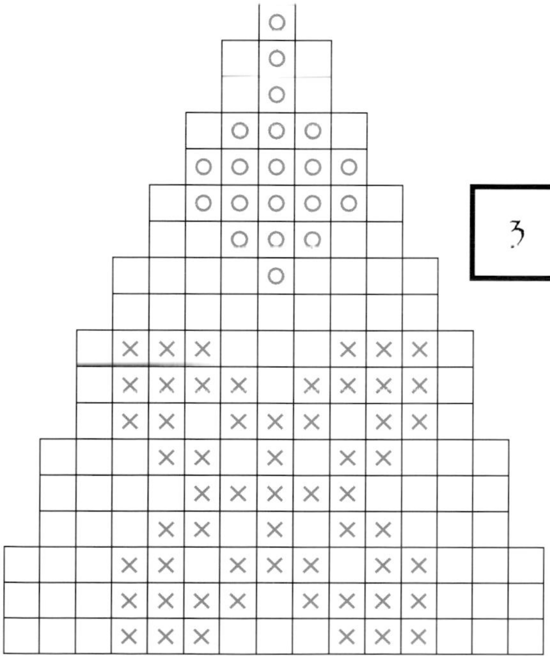

Top

8x

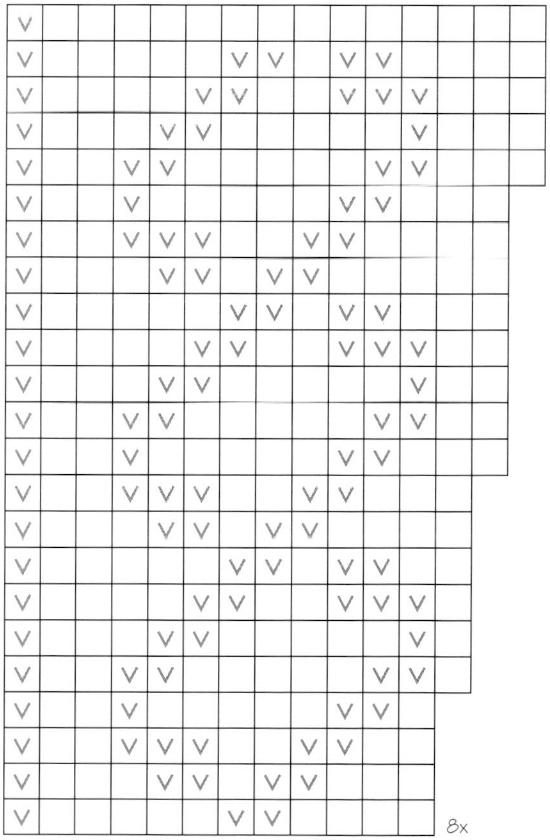

Bottom

8x

12x

Bottom

12x

Top

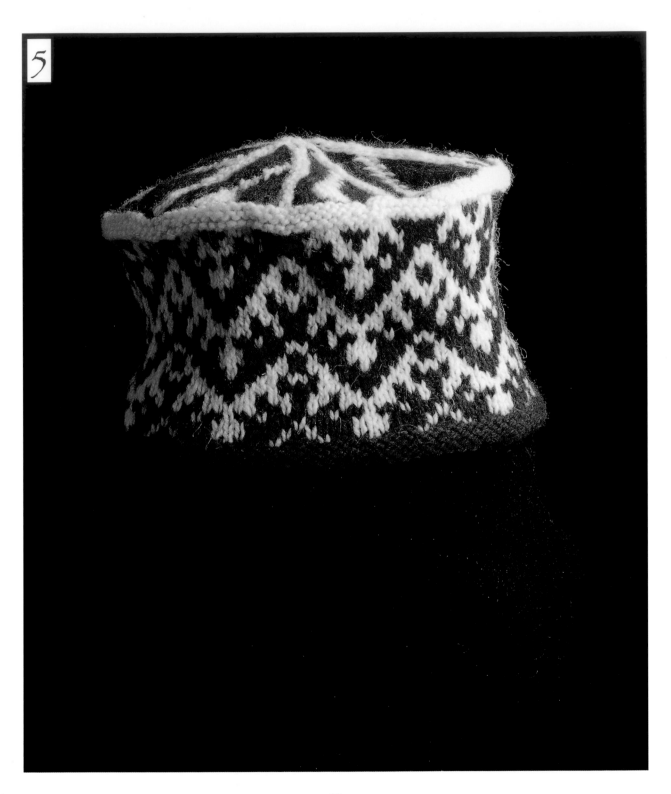

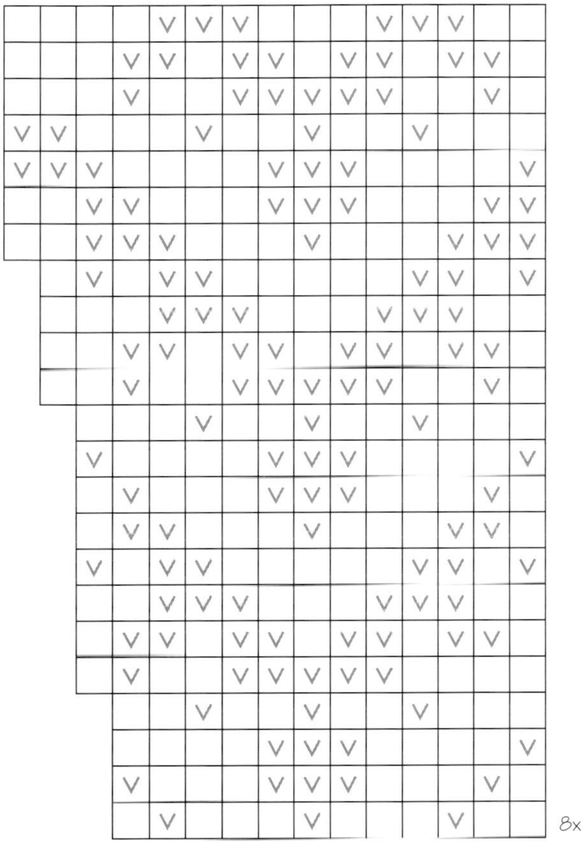
8x

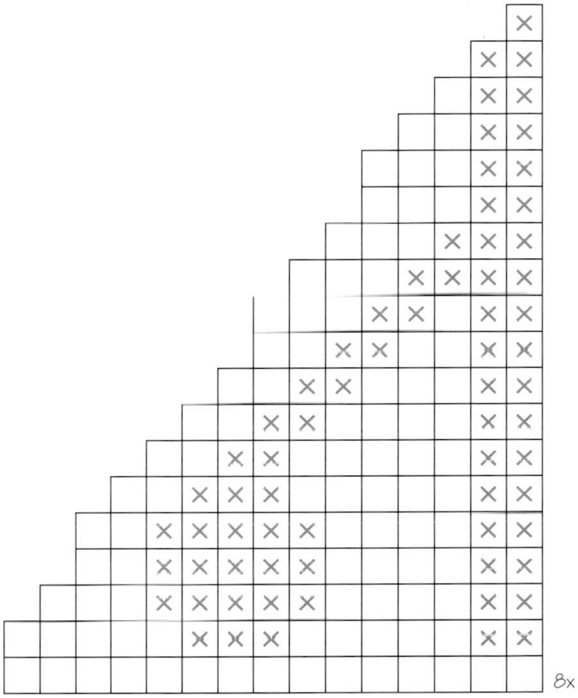
8x

Egyptian
Hats

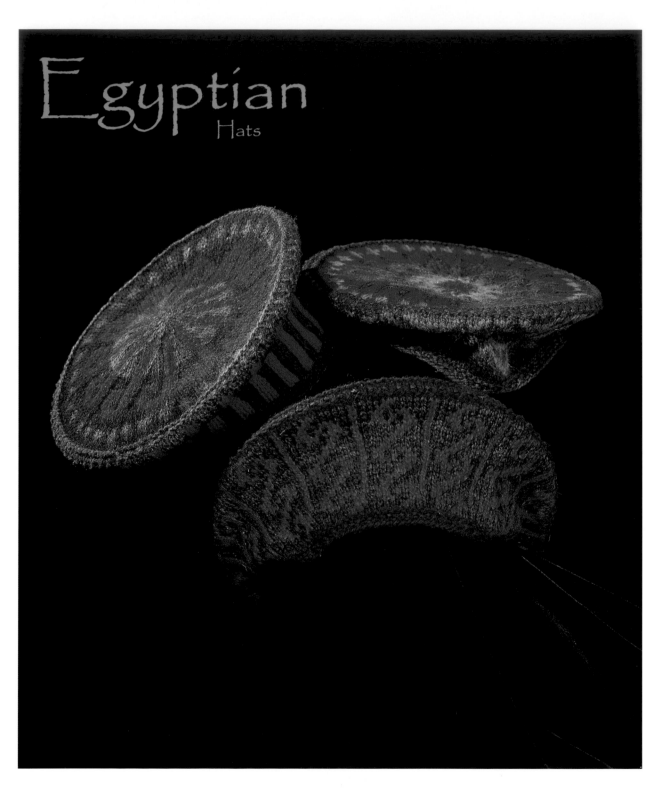

These "Egyptian" hats are composed, basically, of a toque bottom and a beret top. They are far more dramatic on the head than in the hand, and are flattering to a great many faces. A strip of boning in the upper band firmly holds the top out. It isn't absolutely necessary, but I feel more confident with it there.

Boning, the material once used to hold strapless dresses and corsets in place, is now made from plastic and can be purchased in any fabric store in $1/4$-inch or $3/16$-inch (4 - 6 mm) widths. To make a casing on the inside of the hat, use a piece of band-colored yarn on a darning needle. Loosely sew a stitch on the top of the band, a stitch $1/2$ inch (2 cm) away on the bottom of the band, then a half-inch farther on the top of the band. Continue around. Slide the plastic boning under the stitching until it reaches all around plus about 3 inches (7.5 cm) and cut it off. It's not a hard job.

Directions

On the smaller 16-inch (41 cm) circular needle, cast on 96 sts. Join and work band A. Change to larger needle and begin the bottom chart. Repeat the chart around the number of repeats indicated beside the chart, using the lifted increase throughout. When there is a single stich going straight up the side of the chart, increase in the stitch before or after it, as indicated on the chart. When there is no single stitch, increase in the middle, or as close as possible to the middle, of the panel that is enlarging. (When there is an uneven number of sts, you can increase in the middle stitch; when there is an even number, choose one or the other side of the center.)

When you have completed the chart, you should have 144 sts. Work the band again, then follow the top chart. All decreases here are double decreases, except for hat #4, which decreases by K2 tog at the end of every section.

When the chart is finished, run the end of the yarn through the remaining sts and pull the top closed.

Blocking

To block this hat you will need a plate or circle 11-inch (28 cm) in diameter — the same as for the berets. Stretch the top over the circle and steam from the center out. The bottom can be steamed over the tip of an ironing board or sleeve board.

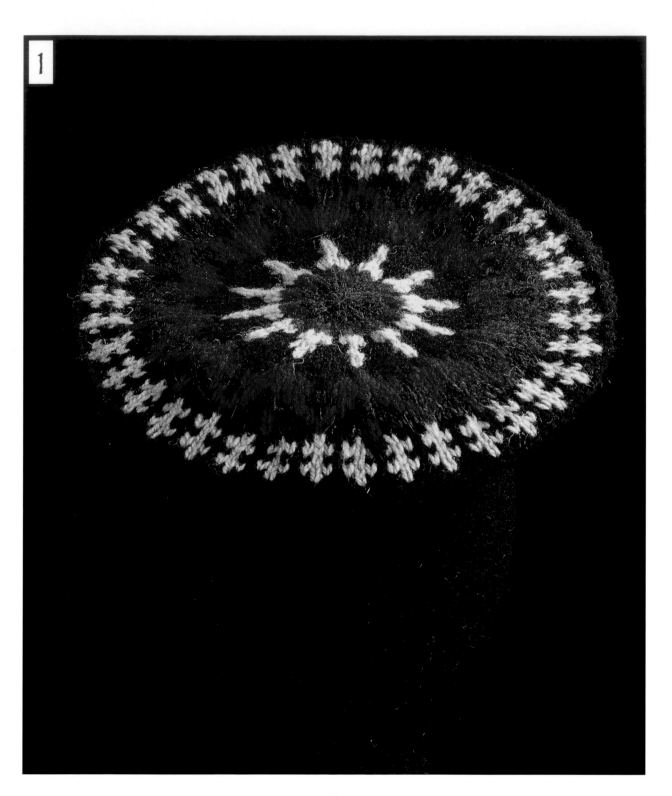

12x

12x

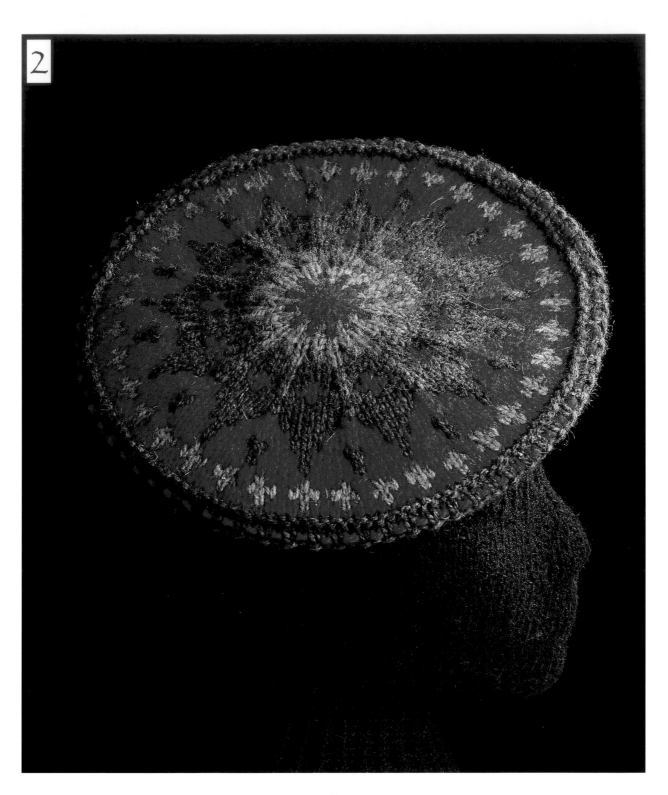

8x

12x

3

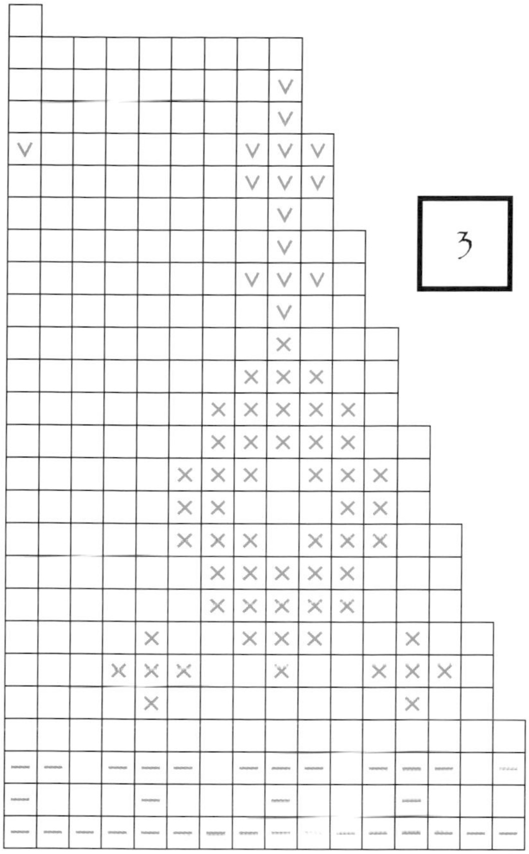

1

9x

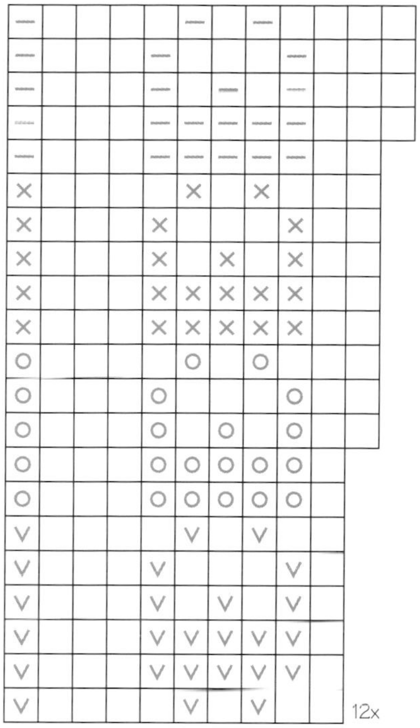

12x

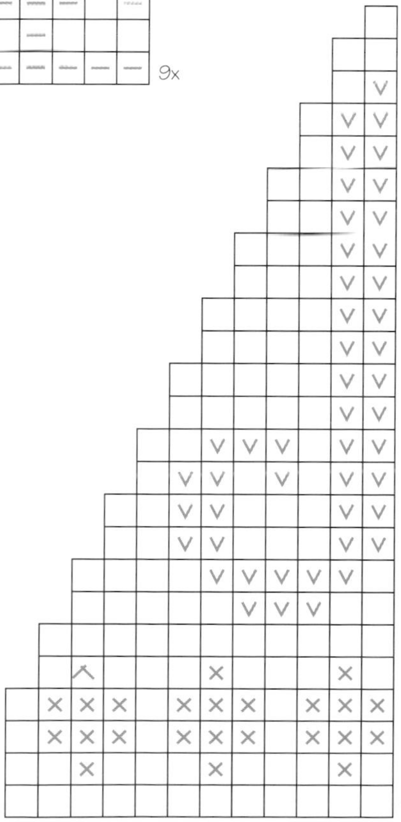

12x

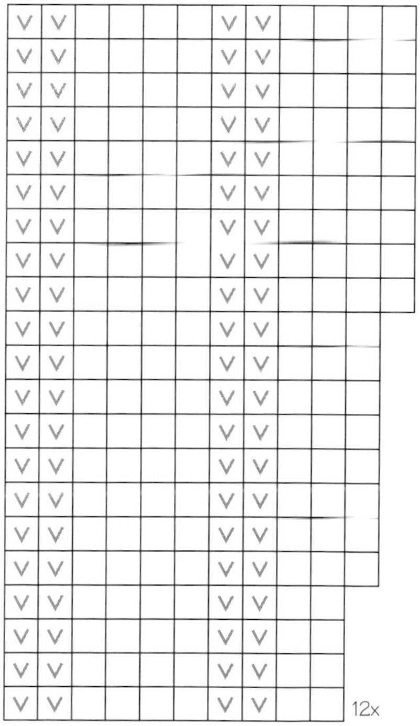

12x

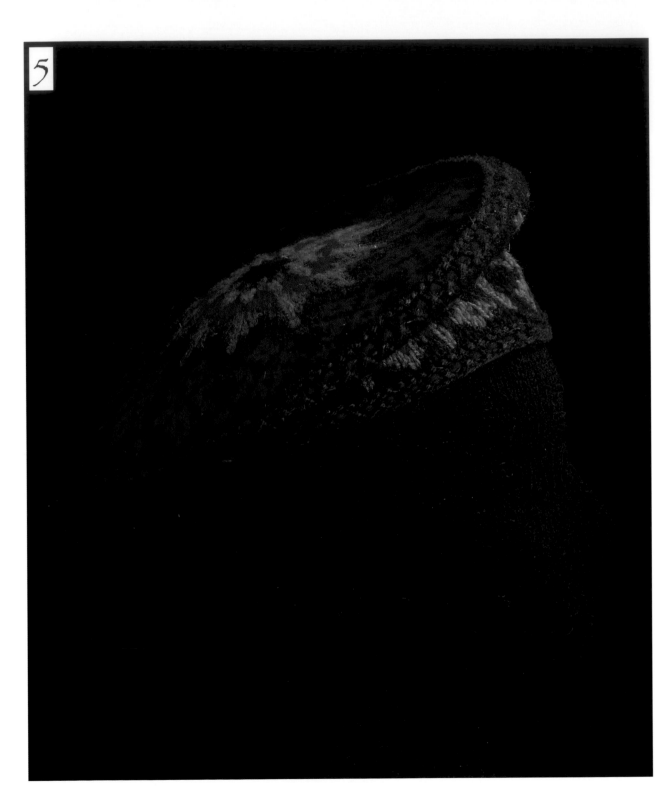

12x

12x

Pentagons

I originally made this hat for a craft show in Wasington, in honor of the locale. It turned out to be versatile and good-looking on many people, so I've put it in this book. Try it both with a point centered on your forehead and with a flat side over your forehead. The difference is surprising. To make the points stand out most sharply, you should skip the band at the end of the bottom chart and put it instead at the widest part, right before you begin to decrease. Hat #5 has been designed this way.

Directions

On a 16-inch (41 cm) circular needle, cast on 100 sts. Work band of choice. Hat #s 1, 2, and 4 use band A; #3 uses band B; and #5 uses band C.

Follow bottom chart. When complete, work band again, except for hat #5.

Begin upper chart. Increase as shown, using the M1 increase. On #5, work band after increasing is completed. Decrease on hat #s 1, 3, and 4 with a R-slanting decrease at the beginning of each section (K2 tog) and a L-slanting decrease at the end of each section (SSK). Use the double decrease on hat #s 2 and 5.

When the chart is finished and you have 10 sts remaining, K2 rnds. Then K2 tog around. Work on 5 sts for 5 or 6 rnds. Pull the tail through the sts and run it into the middle of the point.

Blocking

With the hat upside down on your ironing board, pin each point down. Stretch the hat a bit between points. Make sure that all sides are about the same length, then steam the underside of the pentagon down. Press pretty hard. (Use a press cloth if you're afraid of damaging the wool.) If you have a small enough steamer, or if your iron will fit, put it inside the hat and steam the top from the wrong side.

Remove the pins. When the hat is cool, steam the top over the tip of a sleeve board, and the bottom over the wide end of the sleeve board. If the edges of the pentagon seem soft, steam them one more time. (If there is a band at this edge, as in hat #5, there's no need to worry about the edge.)

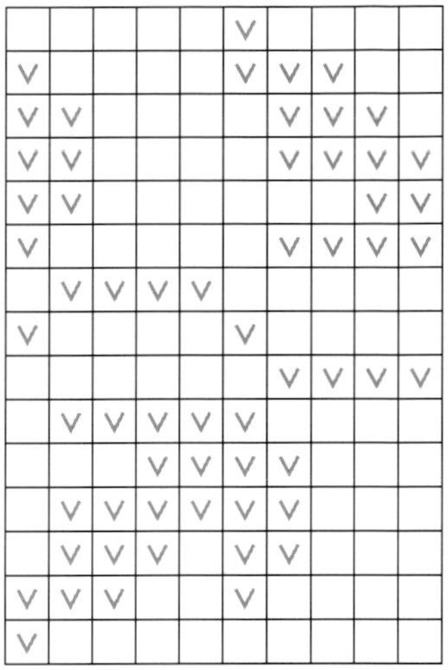

10x

bottom

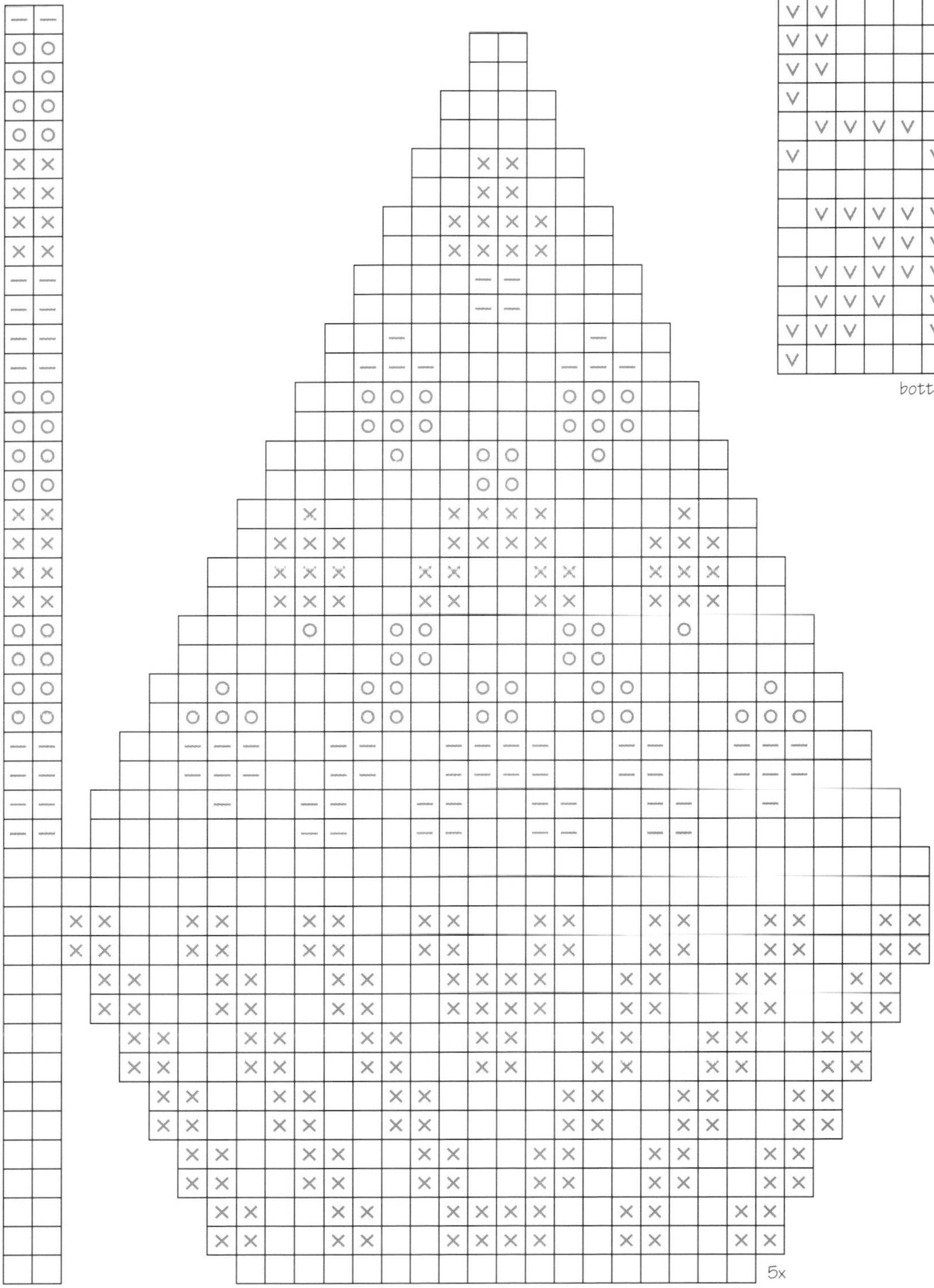

5x

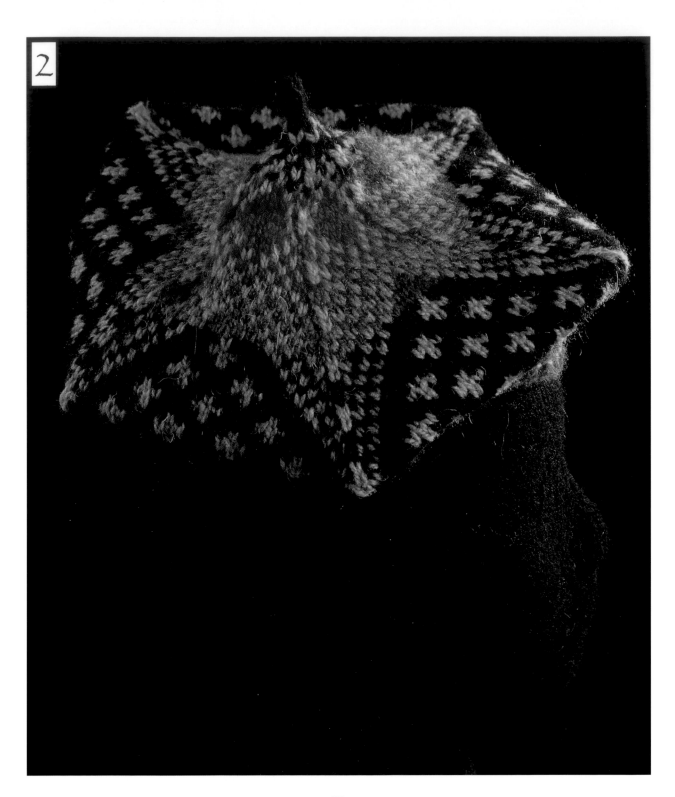

10x

5x

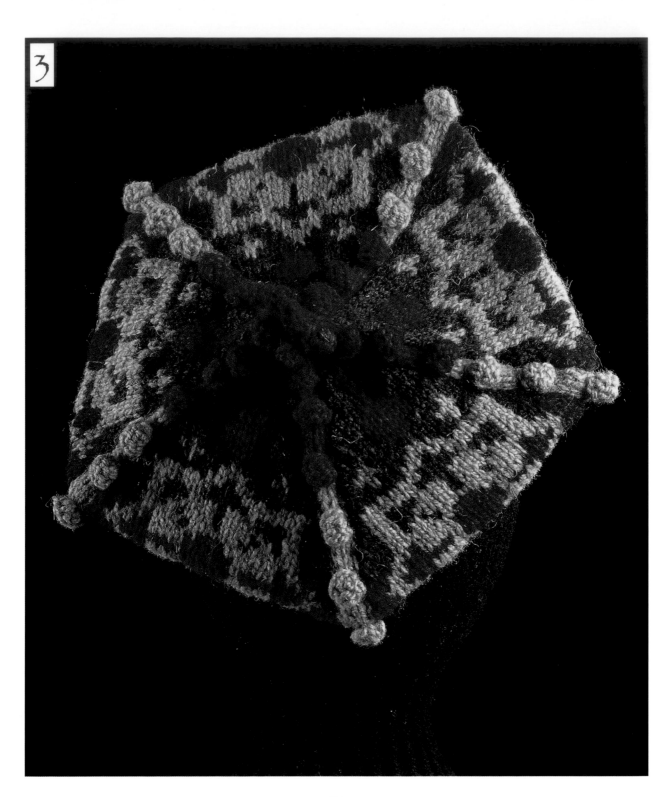

○ indicates a bobble

10x

5x

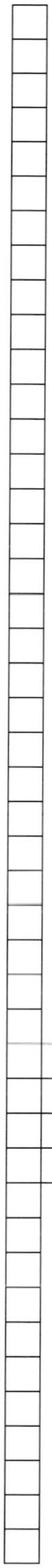

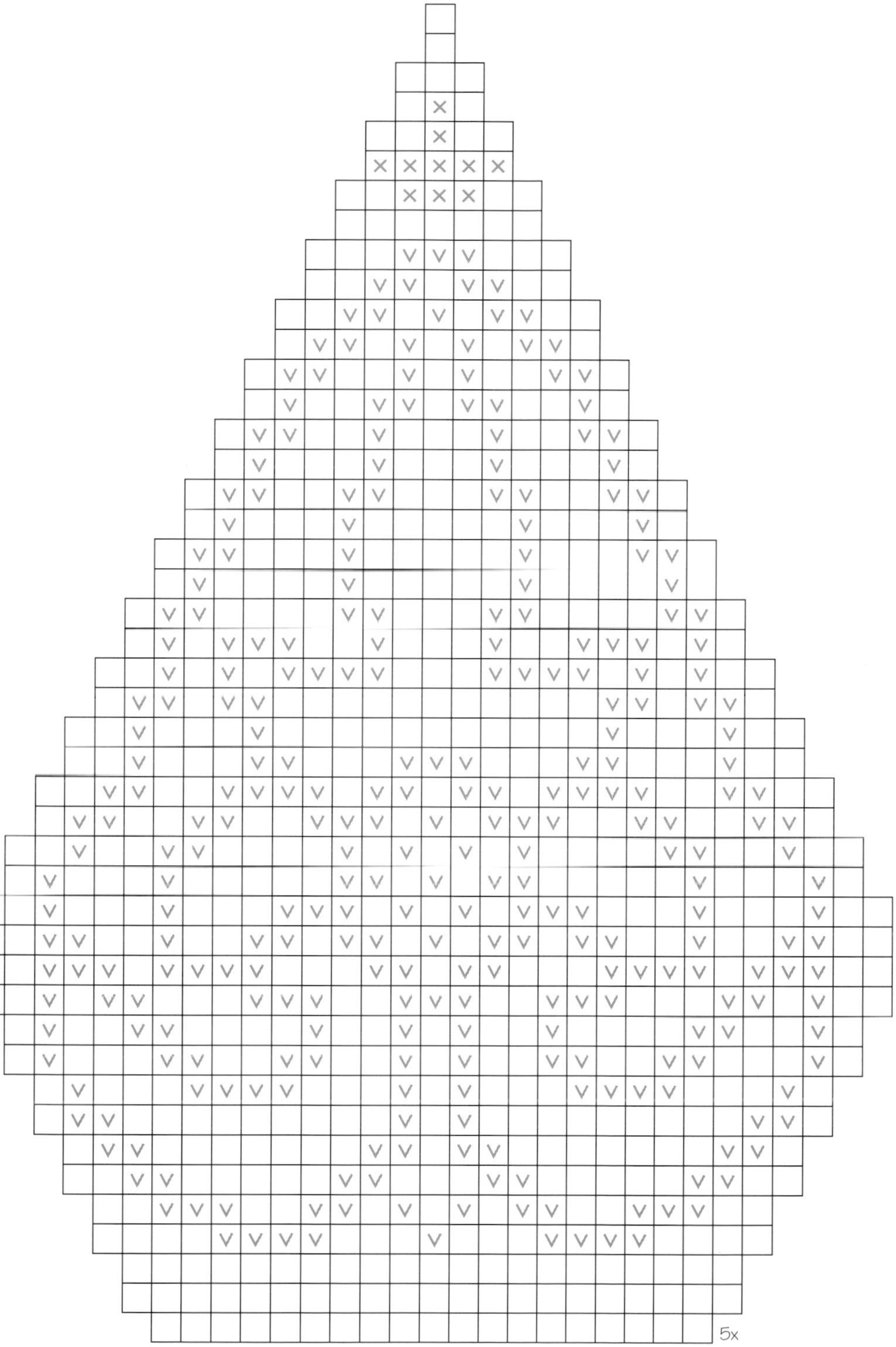

5x

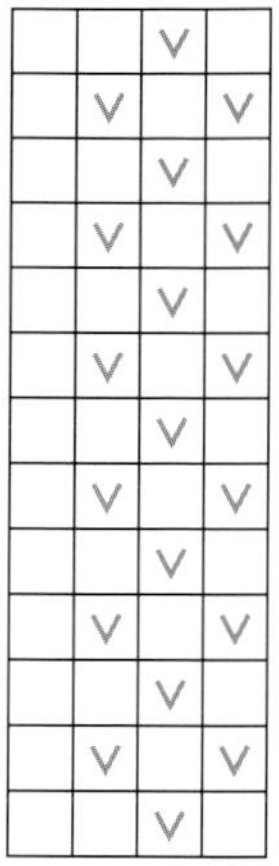

25x

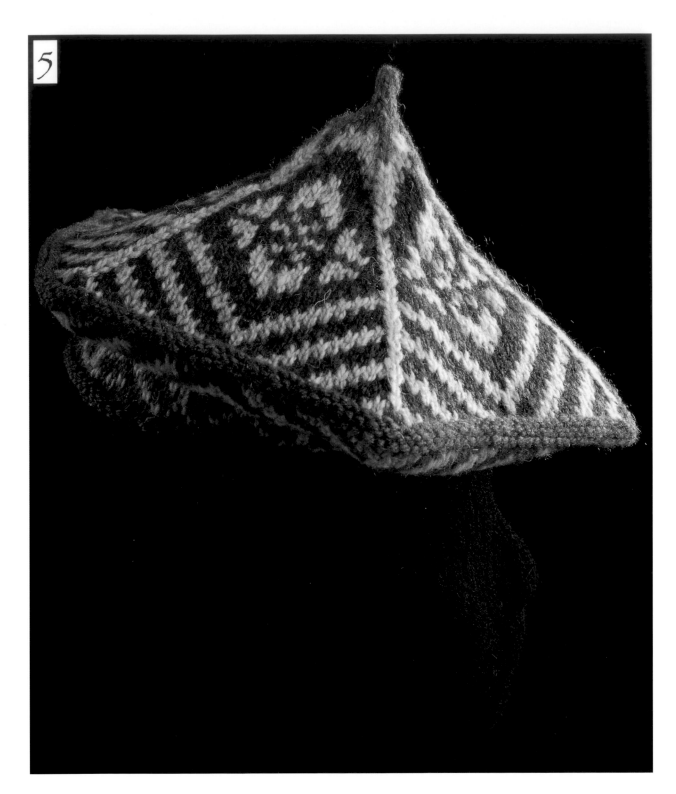

work band here

5x

5x

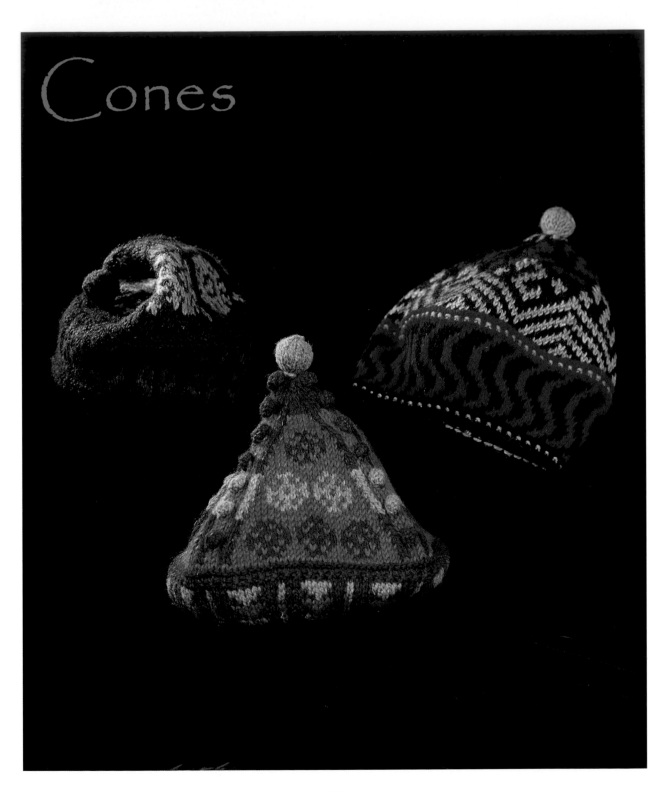

Cones

Cone hats are easy to wear and full of possibilities. Some have shaped bottom bands and some are straight. The straight bottoms are good for small heads, while the shaped bottoms fit a little more loosely and look better on larger heads. The tops are shaped in either four or six sections. All of these hats begin with 96 sts and increase after the second band to 144 sts. The tops and bottoms are completely interchangeable.

Directions

Cast on 96 sts on a 16-inch (41 cm) circular needle. Work band of choice. (All of the bands shown here are Band A.) Follow bottom chart. Work increases on hat #s 1, 2, and 5 with the lifted increase as close as possible to the middle of the space between motifs. On hats 3 and 4 inc. to 144 sts after working chart (K2, M1 around in background color).

When the chart is completed, repeat the band.

Begin the top chart, using the double dec for all except hat #2. Decrease #2 on both sides of the bobble band with L- and R-slanting decreases. (SSK before the band; K2 tog after the band.)

At the top, make a ball or a pom-pom. (For a small child, add a big bell.)

Blocking

The bottom band can be steamed at the tip of an ironing board, but the top is not that easy. The pointed top can be done on the tip of a sleeve board. The lower part does well on a tailor's ham or a rolled-up towel.

24x

6x

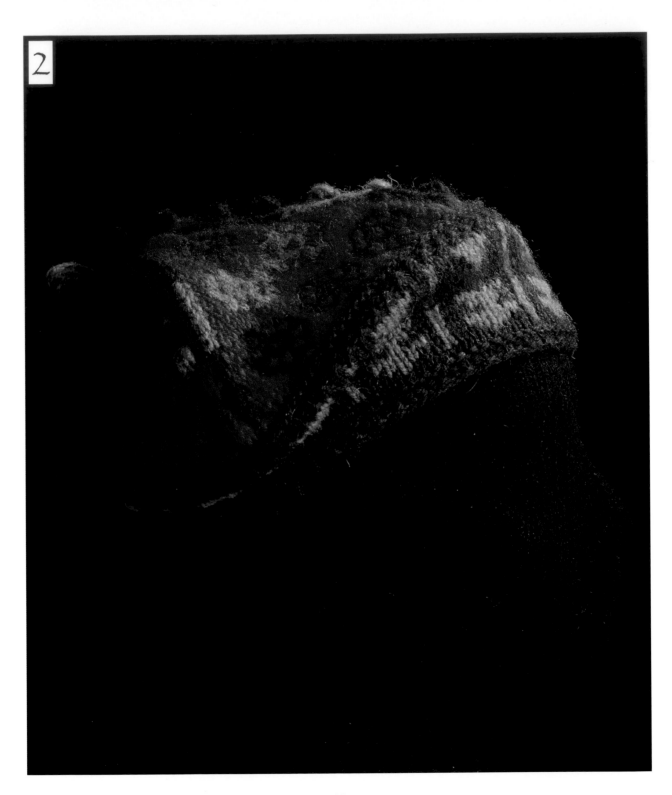

○ indicates a bobble

12x

4x

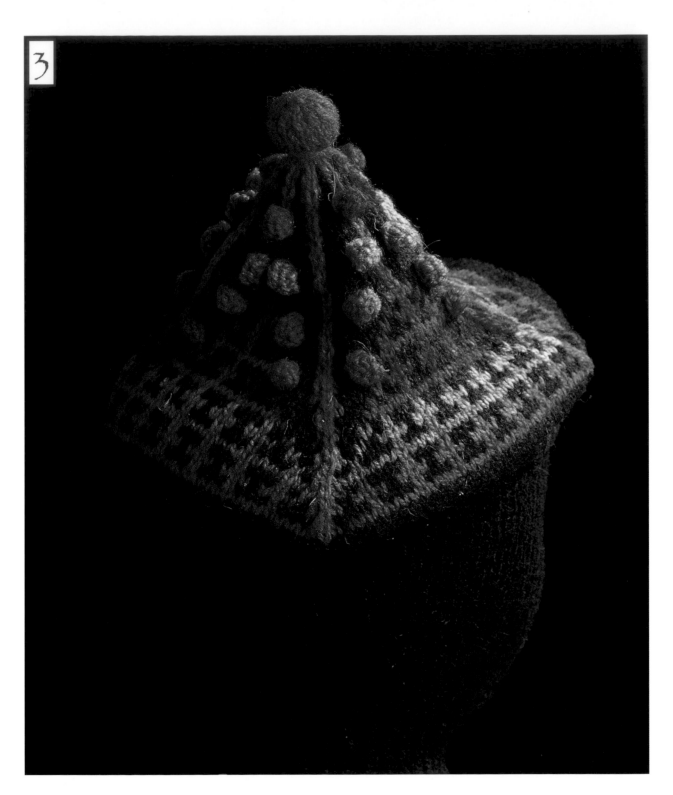

indicates a bobble

8x

4x

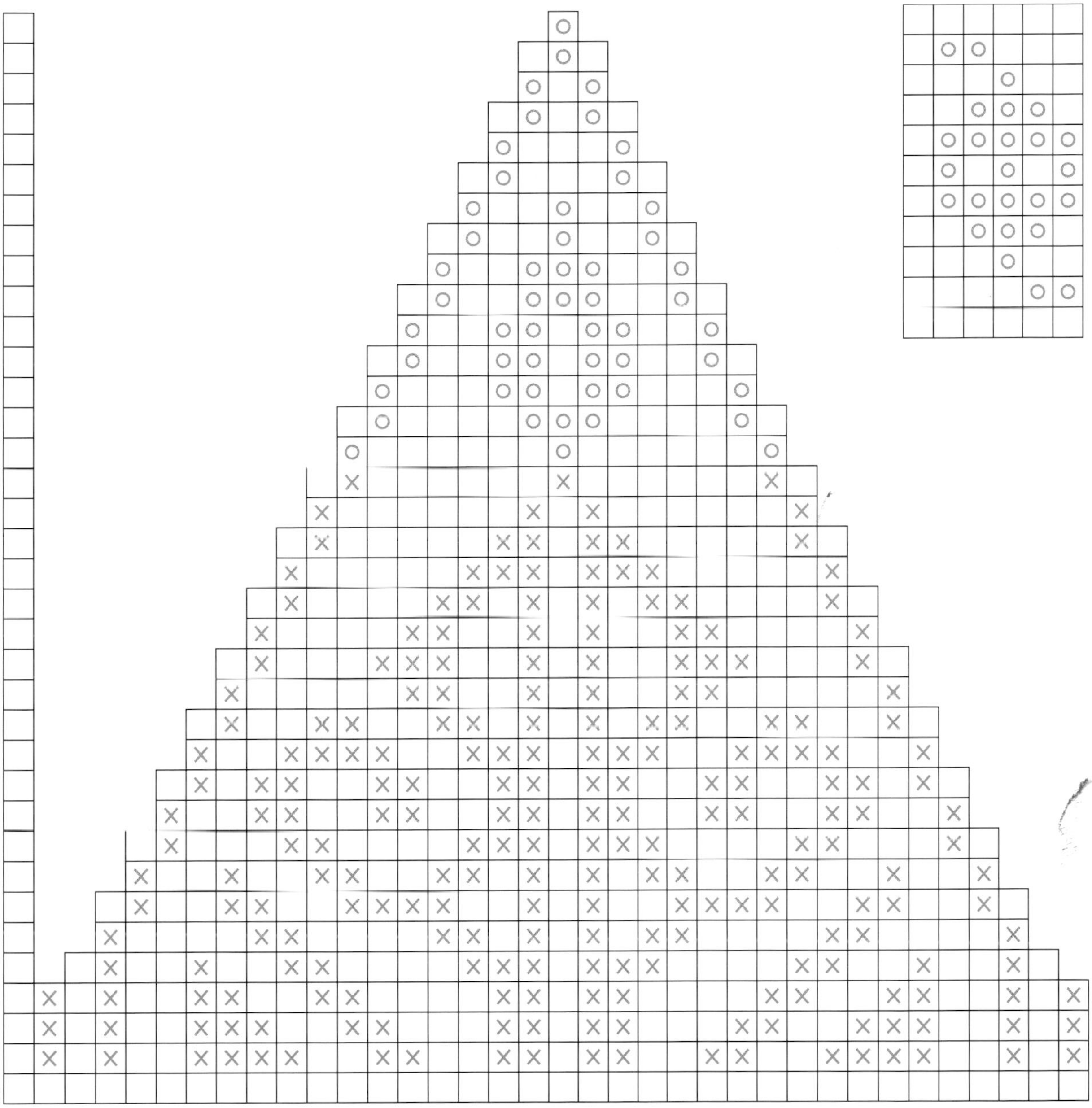

16x

4x

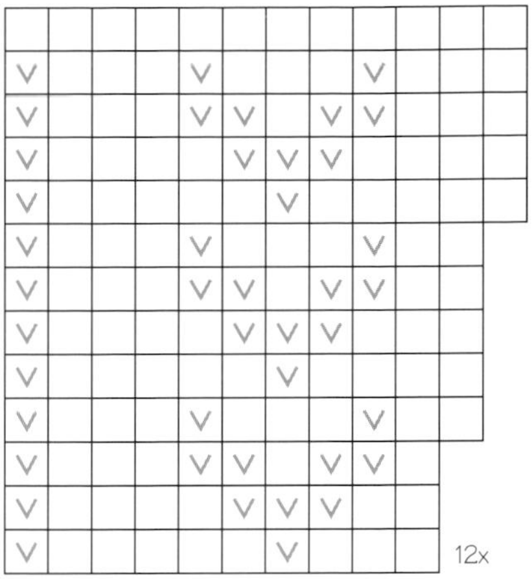

12x

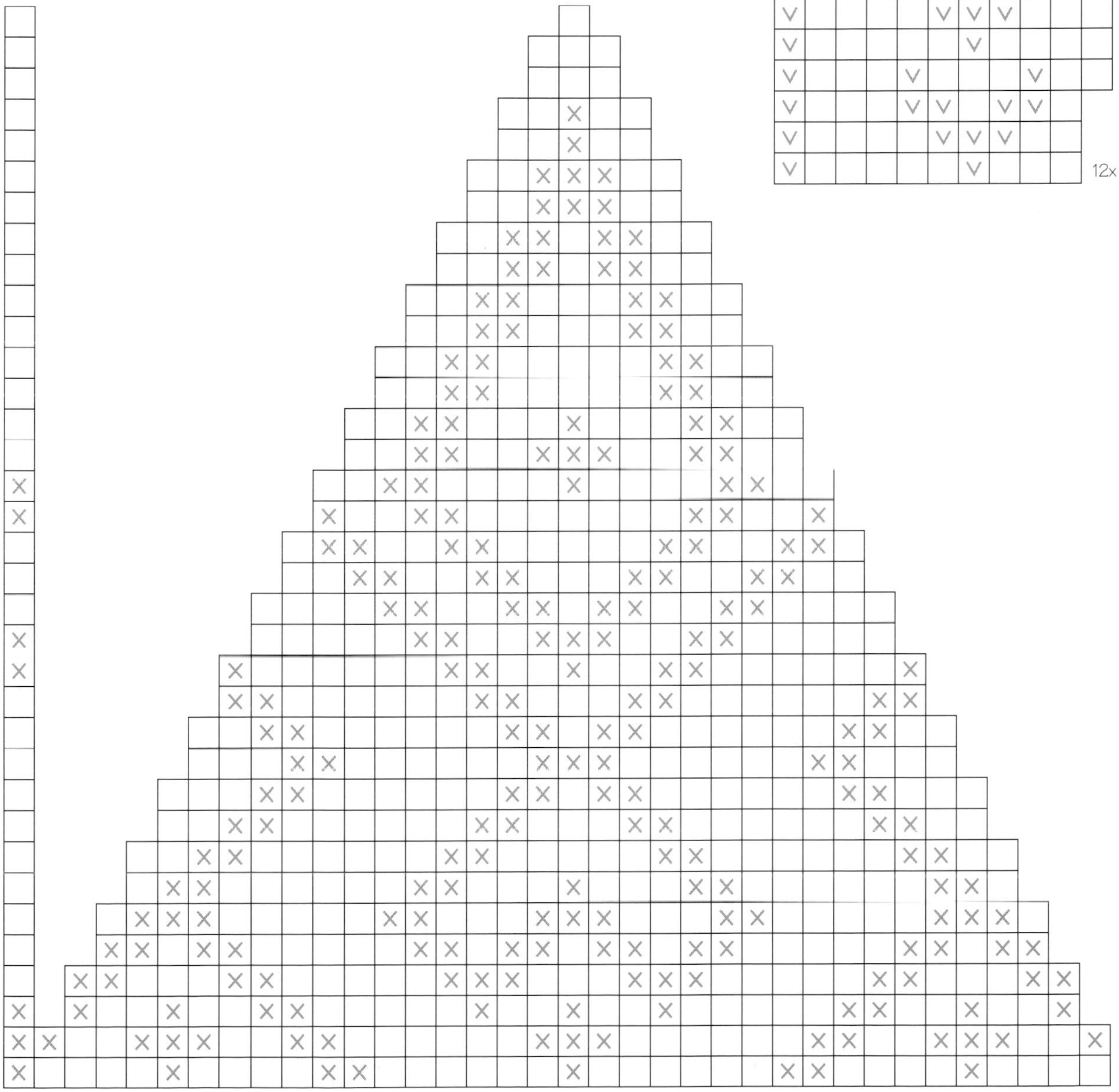

4x

Onion Domes

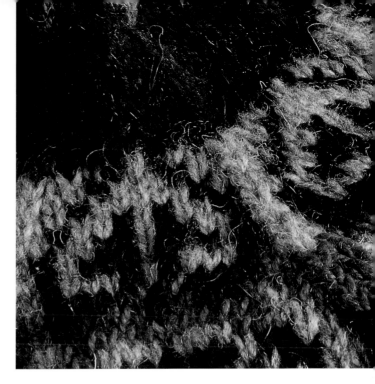

These hats are based on the onion-shaped domes of Russian cathedrals. They look quite decorative on a shelf, propped up by a 10- to 12-inch (25 - 30 cm) bottle underneath. When they are on a head, they tend to look more like a big floppy beret, though when the extra is worn on top of the head instead of on the side or back, the point with the ball stands up. There are two ways to have the whole dome stand up. One is to have luxuriant dreadlocks. The other is to crumple a piece of tissue paper into a ball and put it in the top of the hat. Either way, the effect is dramatic.

Directions

Cast the number of sts indicated by the bottom chart onto a 16-inch (41 cm) circular needle. (That is, the number of sts across the chart multiplied by the number of times the chart is repeated.) For most of the hats, this is 96 sts; for hat #5 it is 98 sts.

Work the desired band. Band A is shown with hat #s 2 and 5; band B with #s 1, 3, and 4; and band C with #4.

Follow the chart for the bottom of the hat. Repeat the band.

Work the top chart. For hat #s 1 and 2, make the increases by M1 and the decreases with L- and R-slanting decreases. For all of the other hats, use double decreases.

When you finish the chart, change to the color you want for the ball. On the first rnd with this color, adjust the number of sts to 8. Then make the ball as instructed on page 11.

Blocking

I block the top few inches (5-8 cm) of this hat by steaming over the tip of a sleeve board. I use a tailor's ham to shape the bulge for steaming. In lieu of a tailor's ham, you can stuff a rolled-up towel into the hat and steam over it. The shape is defined well enough by the increasing and decreasing and doesn't need forcing. The bottom of the hat steams easily over the ironing board tip or the sleeve board.

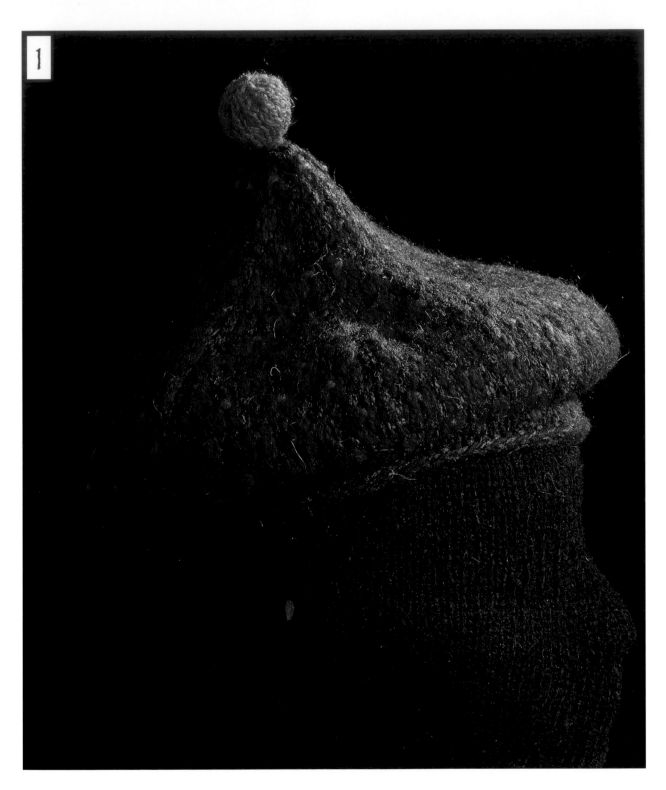

V These stitches are knit, but the stitches over them on the next round are purled.

8x

6x

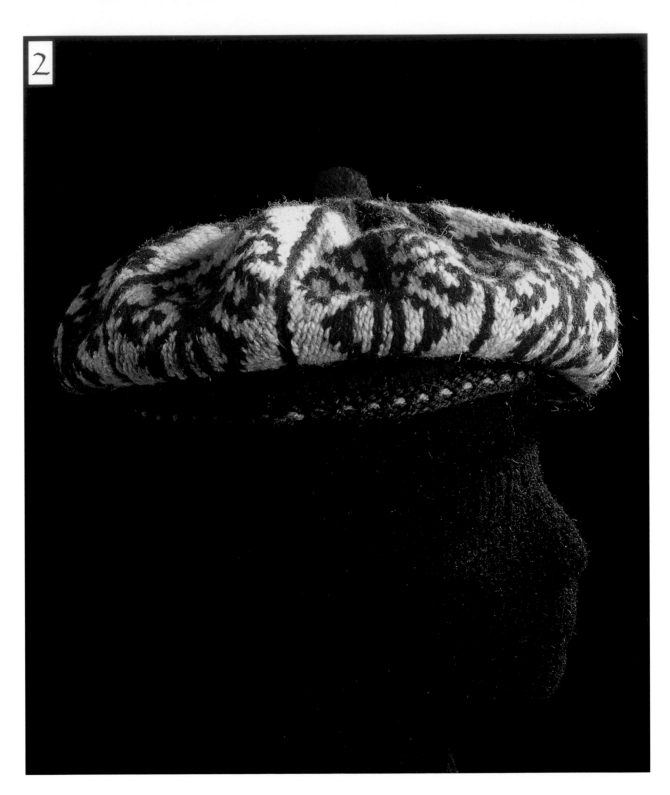

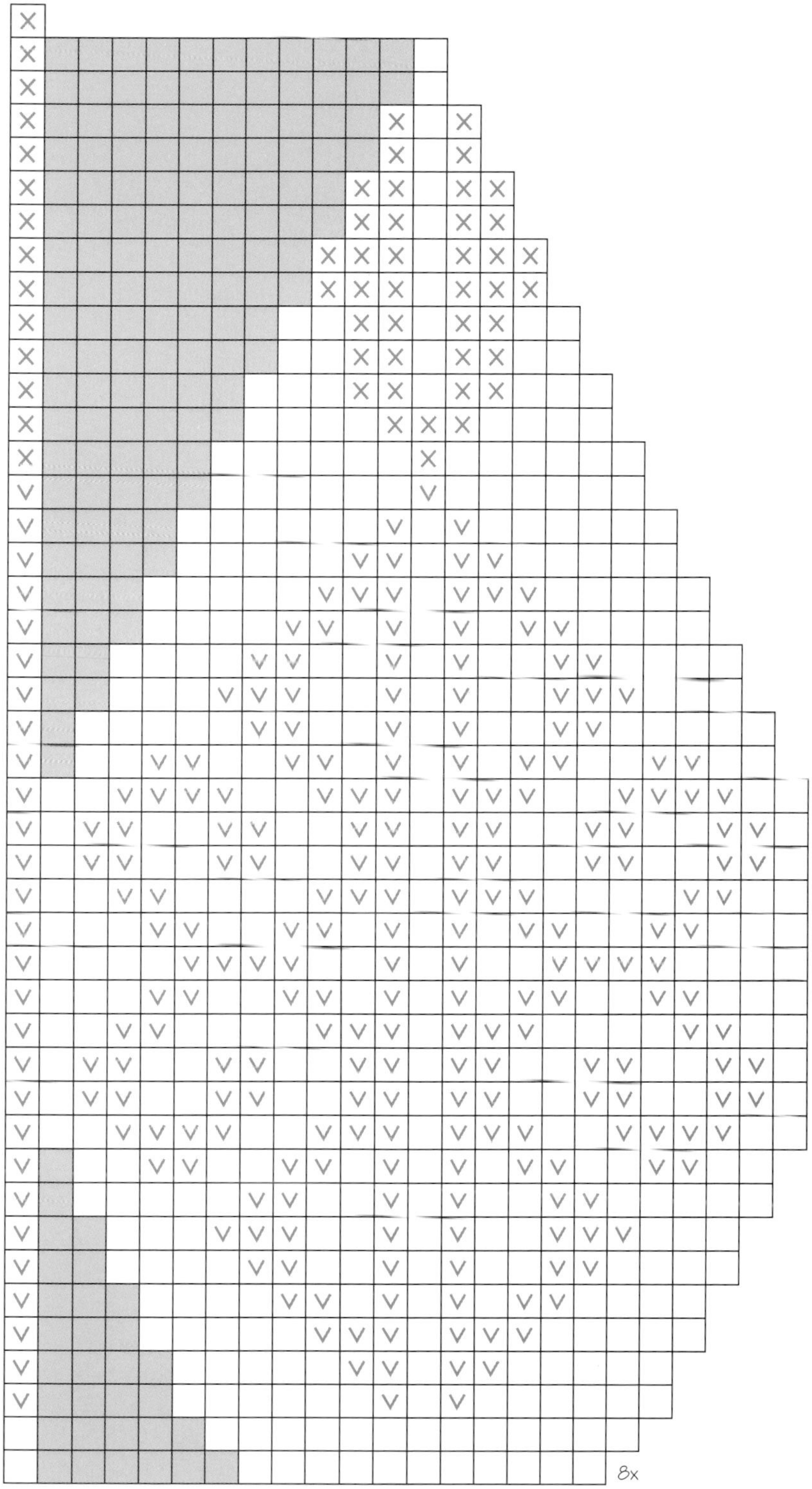

8x

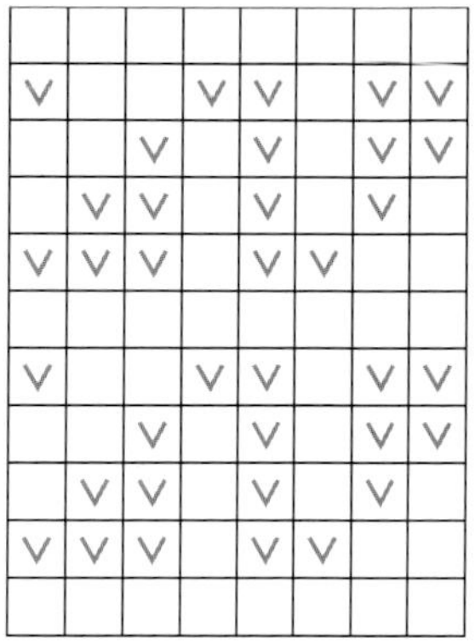

12x

12x

8x

12x

On the first round of this chart,
inc. to 144sts (K2M1 around)

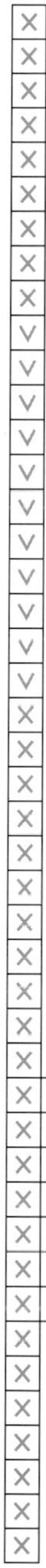

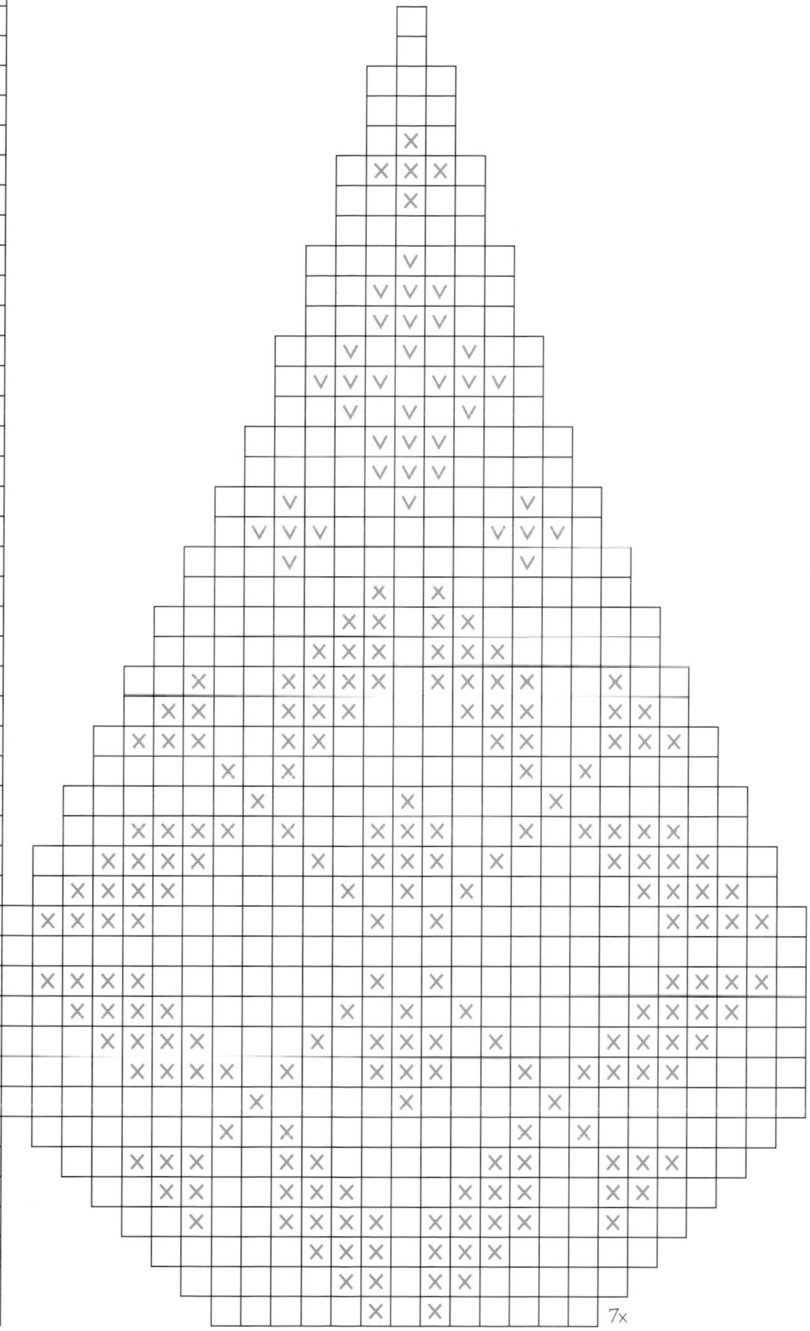
7x

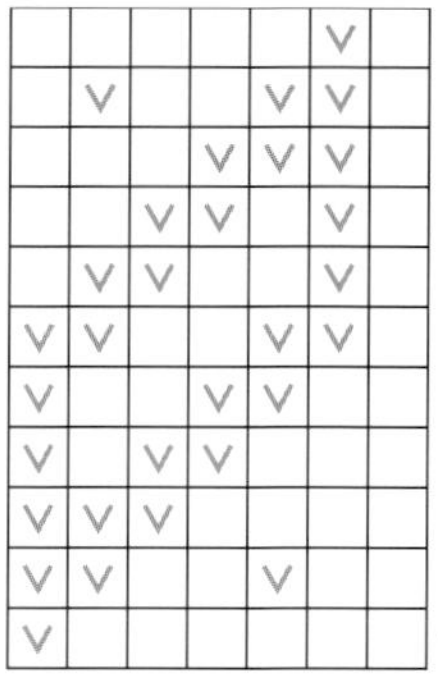
14x

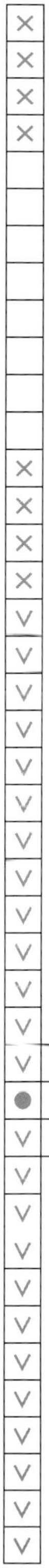

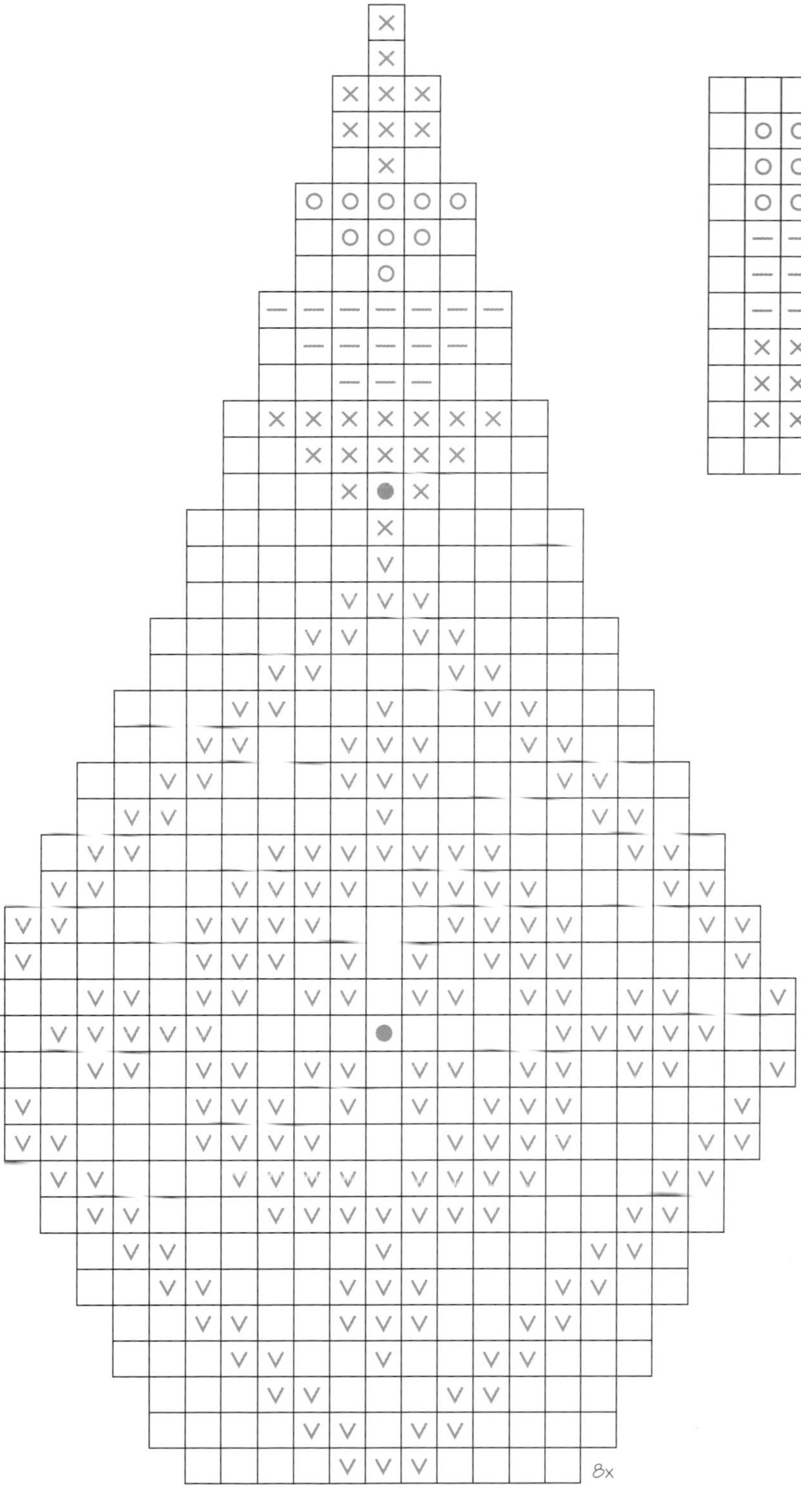
8x

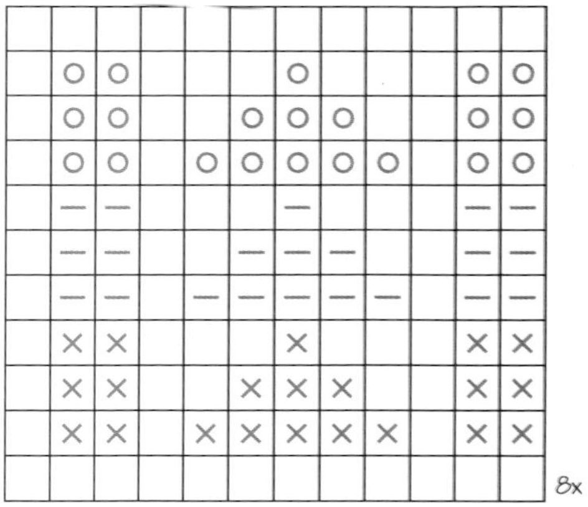
8x

Stacked
Hats

tacked hats are actually double or triple berets. All of the triple ones shown here can be made double and vice versa. The triple is the most dramatic; the double a third less work. They remind everyone of *The Cat in the Hat*, and hence they make people merry.

One word of warning: Hat #4 is an attractive hat but it isn't an easy pattern. Do not try it if you aren't adept at stranded knitting. There's no reason to discourage yourself. The others are all pretty simple.

Directions

On a 16-inch (41 cm) circular needle, cast on 96 sts. Work 3 ridges of garter stitch.

Follow the bottom chart. When there are single increases in a rnd, use the lifted increase. When there are paired increases (one on either side of a stitch that does not change) use the M1.

When you reach the blank line on the chart, P1 rnd in the colors established. (Hat #4 is an exception to this. On that hat, K1 rnd in background color, then P 1 rnd in background color.)

Continue with the chart. For single decreases, K2 tog. For paired decreases, K2 tog at the beginning of a section and SSK at the end.

When you have finished the chart, repeat it. When you have finished the repeat, work half of it again. After the P rnd, go to the top chart.

Work the top chart. Finish off the last sts by pulling the end of the yarn through them.

Blocking

Block this hat as though you are working with three berets. First place a plate or other circle in the top. Steam the top and underneath side. Move the circle down to the second layer and steam it, then move to the first layer. Lay the hat flat and steam it again. Use a press cloth if you're worried about harming the fibers.

Another option is to wet down the hat, get as much moisture out as you can, lay it flat, and put something heavy on it for a day. Take the weight off and allow the hat to finish drying.

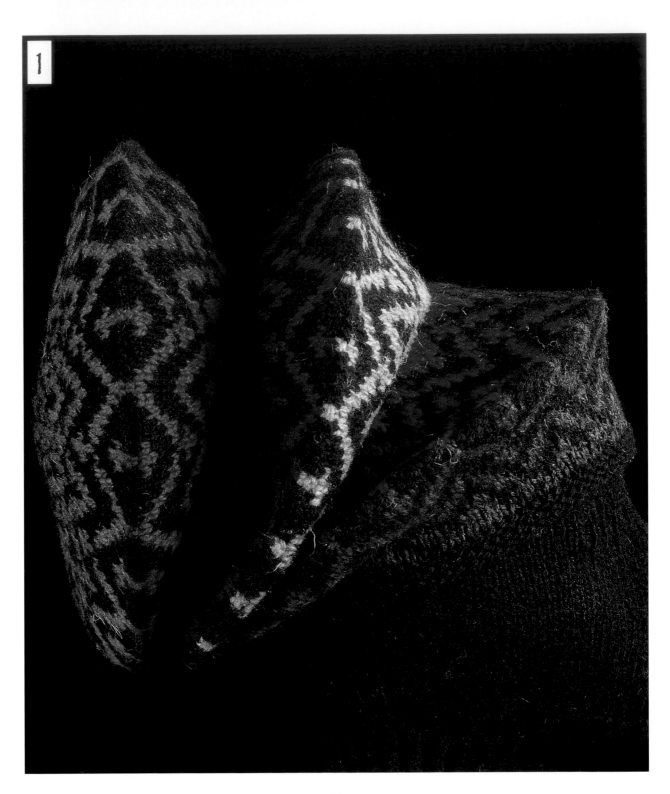

bottom

12x

top

12x

12x

12x

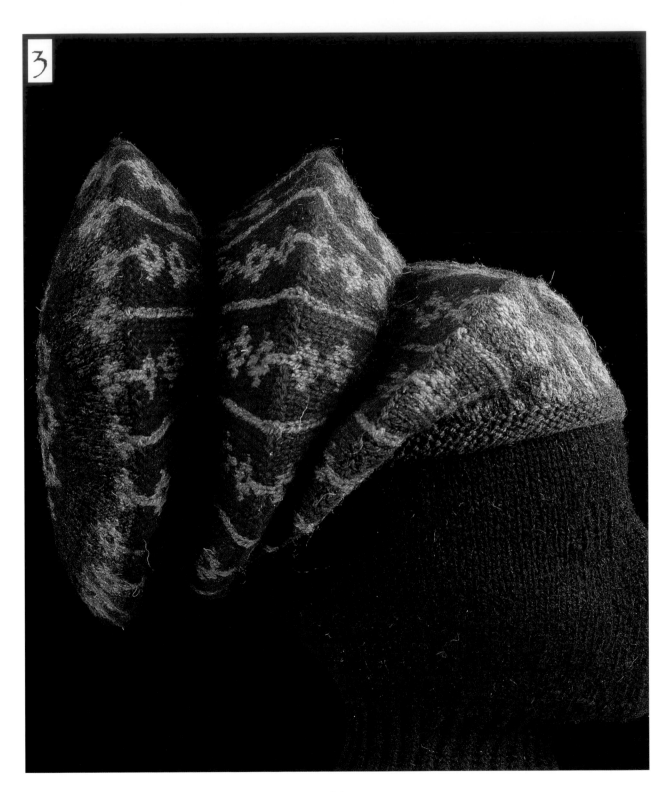

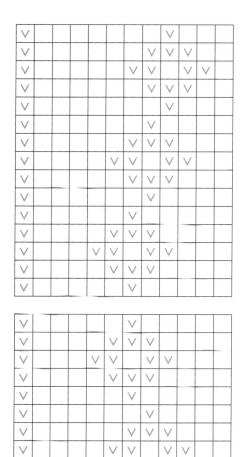

bottom

top

12x

12x

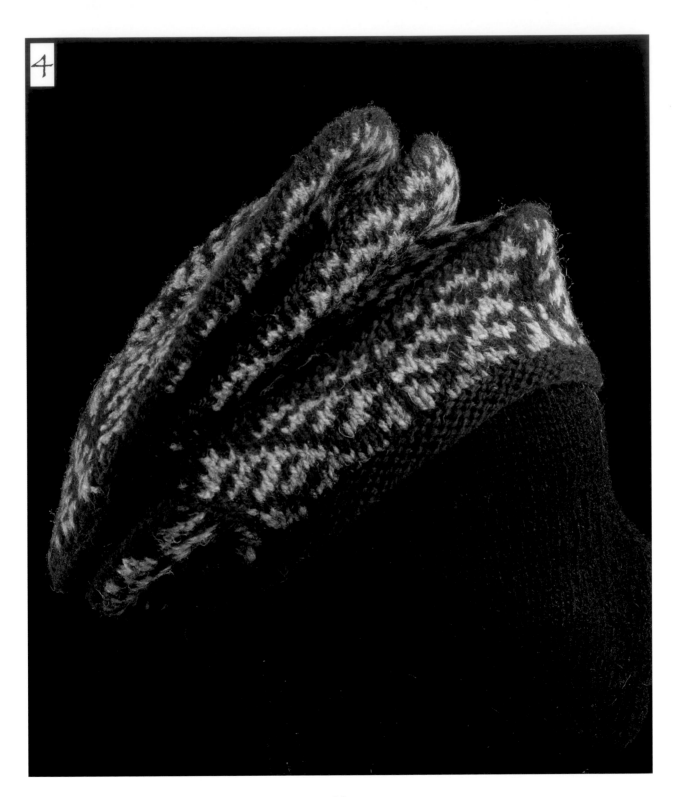

top

4x

bottom

4x

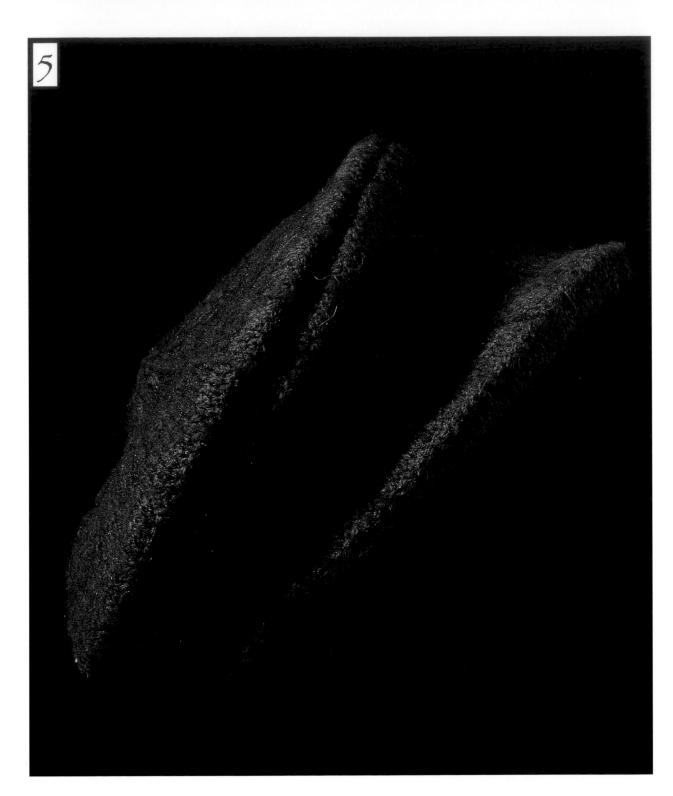

bottom

12x

12x

S tar hats are probably the most dramatic hats in this book. They can be worn a number of different ways. If the bottom layer is tucked under, the head becomes surrounded in a triangular bonnet. Placed straight, the head is surrounded by a star. If you place the hat straight and then pick up the center top and pull it to one side, the effect is both goofy and wonderful. Once, at a craft show, someone did just that and walked out of my booth wearing the hat. In the next half-hour, six people came in wanting one too.

They are fun to make, but more work than most of the other varieties.

Directions

On a 16-inch (41 cm) circular needle, cast on 84 sts. Work 5 ridges of garter st. On the next rnd, inc to 126 sts (K2 M1 around). Work bottom chart using M1 increases. At the end of the color pattern there are 4 rnds of solid color. For these, work 2 ridges of garter st. Continue with the decreasing part of the chart. Use R-slanting dec at beginning of chart and L-slanting dec at end of chart

When the whole chart is finished, break off the yarns. Slip 21 sts from the left side to the right. Start the next rnd here, in the middle of a side of the bottom triangle. Repeat the whole chart.

When the large chart is finished for the second time, K1 rnd with ground color, decreasing 10 sts each section (K2, K2 tog across, ending K2) in addition to the corner decreases.

Work smaller chart to finish hat. Run end of yarn through remaining sts and pull tight.

Blocking

With the hat upside down, pin the top at three points to make a triangle. (The sides will remain slightly curved.) Steam the sides of the triangle. Fit your steamer inside the hat to steam the top if you can. Then pin down the other triangle at its corners and steam it. Let the hat sit until cool. Unpin and turn over. Steam first the bottom layer and then the top.

It's also possible to wet down the whole hat and pin it right side up by all six corners and let it dry in place.

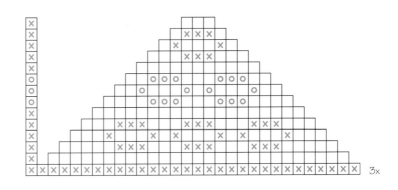

3x

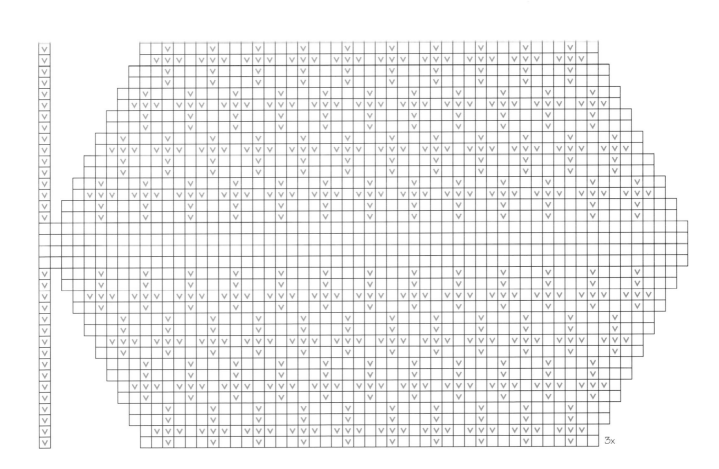

3x

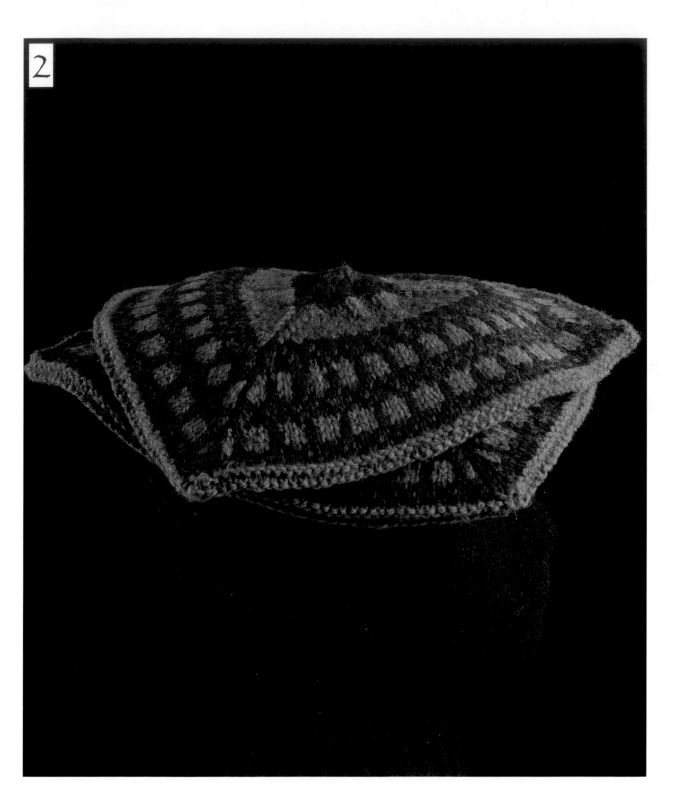

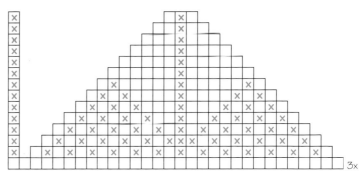

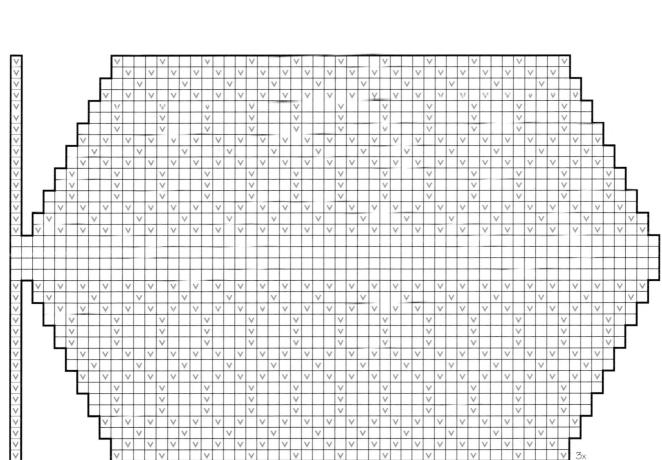

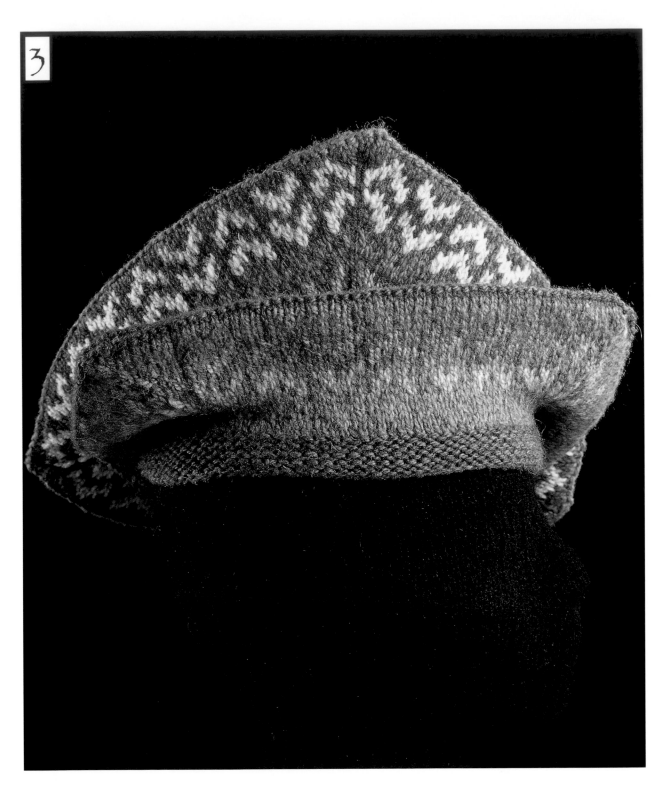

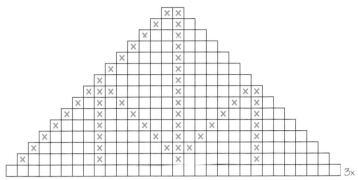

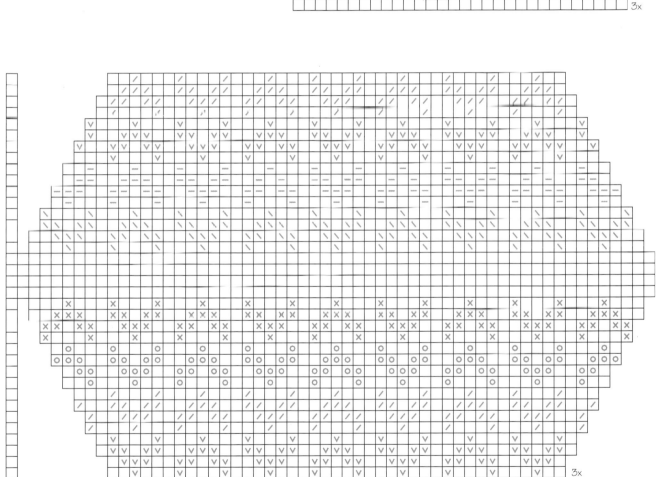

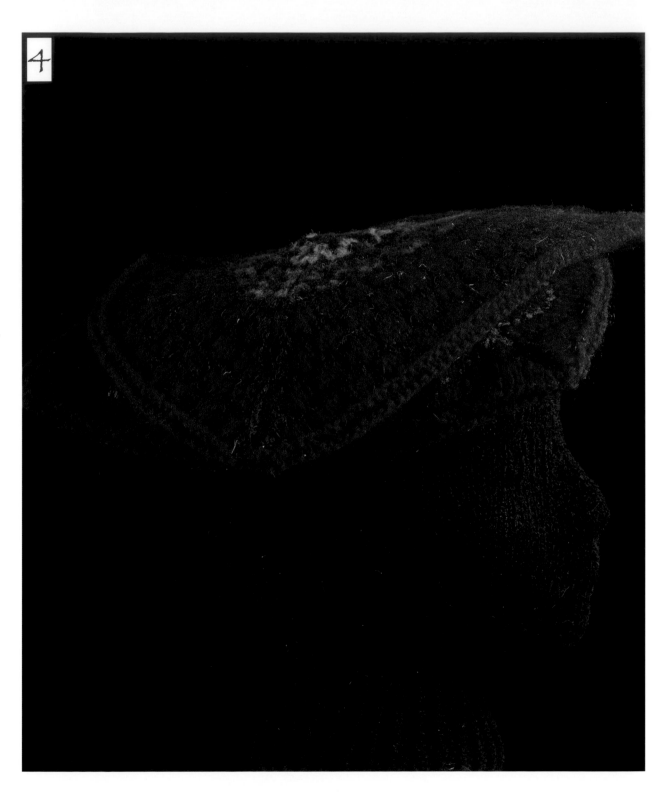

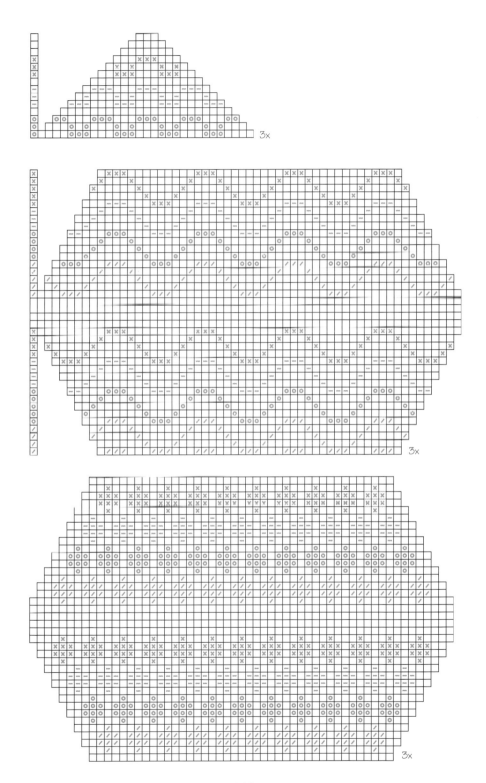

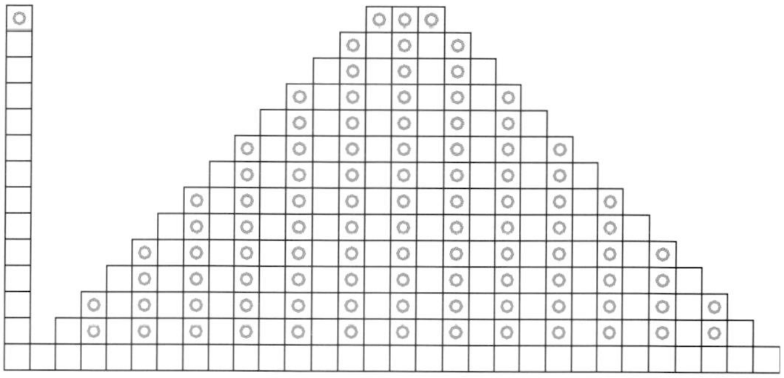
3x

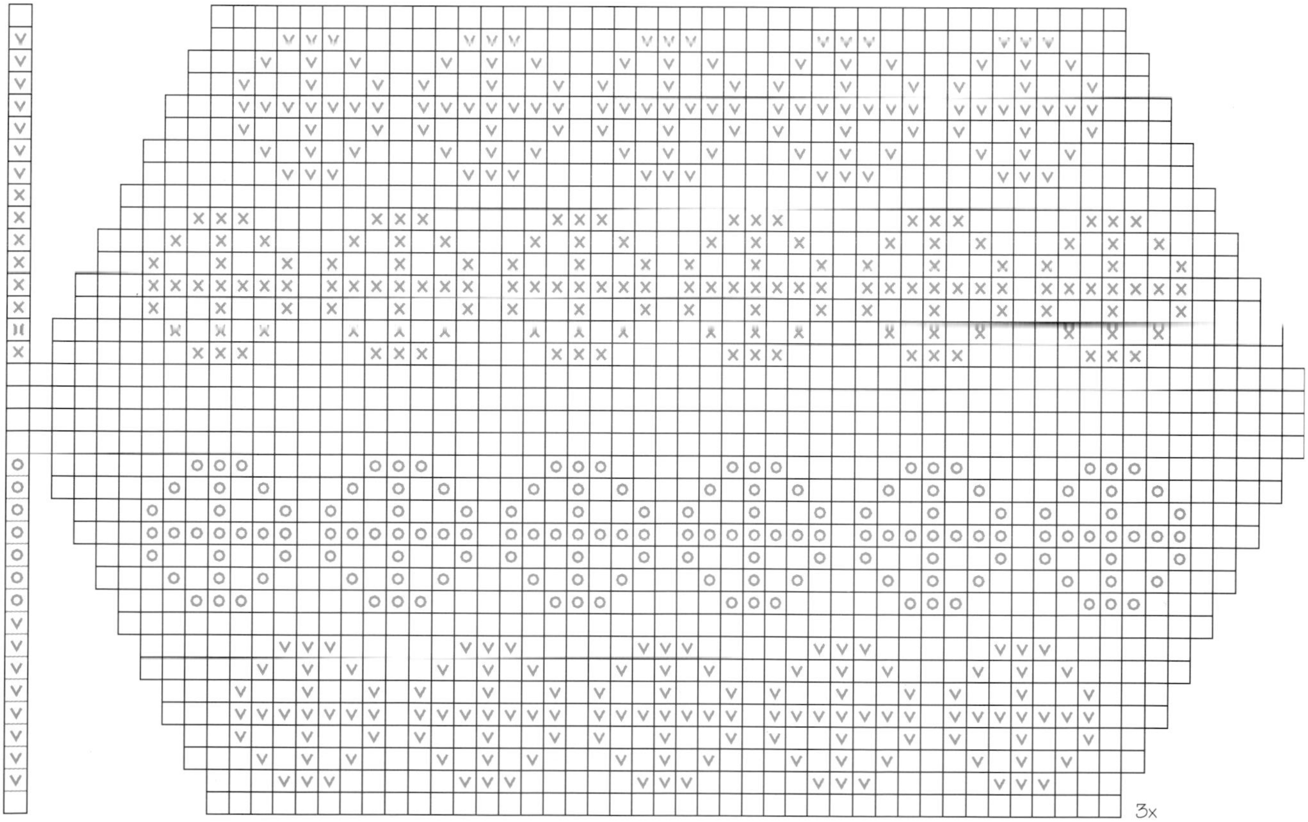
3x

Index